# TRAVELLING ON THE VICTORIAN RAILWAY

## TRAVEL IN THE EARLY DAYS OF STEAM

ANTHONY DAWSON

First published 2017

Amberley Publishing
The Hill, Stroud,
Gloucestershire, GL5 4EP

www.amberley-books.com

ISBN: 978 1 4456 6774 4 (print)
ISBN: 978 1 4456 6775 1 (ebook)

British Library Cataloguing in Publication Data.
A catalogue record for this book is available from the British Library.

Typeset in 10pt on 13pt Celeste.
Typesetting by Amberley Publishing.
Printed in the UK.

# Contents

# Acknowledgements

As is customary, I would like to thank all those who have helped with the writing and preparation of this book: Andy Mason for his continued unfailing support for my writing; the railway volunteers at MSI, Manchester; Matthew Jackson for photos; and to Peter Chatham and Stephen Weston (who produce a range of exquisite 7 mm scale models of early railway rolling stock) of the LNWR Society for their encouragement and for permission to reproduce drawings of early London & Birmingham Railway carriages.

# CHAPTER 1

# Preparing to Travel

The year is 1838, and, following one of the coldest winters on record (-19°C), the year dawns as one of great change. In April, Brunel's giant paddle steamer, SS *Great Western*, crosses the Atlantic from Avonmouth to New York in fifteen days, heralding a regular transatlantic steamship crossing. Queen Victoria is crowned at Westminster Abbey in June, and the Newcastle & Carlisle Railway opens in the same month, as does the first section of the Great Western Railway.

The fastest means of conveyance until this point had been the mail coach, which was introduced in 1784. By 1830, the Manchester Mail took nineteen hours to cover the 187 miles from London; the Liverpool Mail covered 203 miles in twenty hours and fifty minutes; and the Holyhead Mail travelled its 261 miles in twenty-six hours and fifty-five minutes. Travelling to Edinburgh by mail coach was a mammoth, bottom-numbing forty hours over rutted roads in a tiny compartment devoid of heating or lighting.

From September 1838, it becomes possible to travel by train from London (Euston) to Manchester or Liverpool via Birmingham in eight and a half hours. This journey is made possible through the co-operation of the Liverpool & Manchester, Grand Junction and the London & Birmingham railways. Though slow by today's standards, the journey from London to Manchester or Liverpool was a phenomenal feat of engineering and speed.

## Stagecoach versus Railway Coach

For a prospective traveller wishing to travel north from London to Liverpool or Manchester in 1837, the journey could be completed by road or by a coastal sailing vessel – a prospect that was only for the hardy.

To make the journey by road, our traveller would have the choice of travelling direct to Liverpool or Manchester using the system of mail coaches. The Post Master General approved routes, but the provision of service was contracted to outside coach proprietors. In addition to the Royal Mail, four to six passengers could be carried at a maximum speed of 10 mph. The *Edinburgh Evening Courant* (Monday 29 June 1829) thought a proposed acceleration of the mail coach was neither practical nor safe:

> The increase of speed, still being so strongly pressed ... is assumed to be easy ... the practicabilities of a mail coach carrying seven passengers besides coachmen and guard, with passengers' luggage, many large sacks of letters, newspapers, and Parliamentary papers ... of great weight on the roof, over and above what are contained in the place appropriated for the mail bags, which has become insufficient for them.

The mail coaches are timed from 9¼, to 9½ and even 10 miles an hour – the last pace raises the actual speed while travelling to near 11 miles, to cover the change of horses, the change of bags ... and the delivery and taking up of passengers. It is conceived that 10 miles an hour ... is therefore the highest speed at which a mail coach should be timed, but only in daylight and on the best roads...

A traveller could engage the services of any number of stagecoach proprietors, such as Messrs. A. Paterson & Co., who commenced running in October 1800. Paterson ran both the Royal Mail coach and two stagecoaches on the London–Manchester run, *The Cornwallis* and *The Defiance,* at a cost of £3 3s inside and £1 11s 6d outside, which were 'well lighted and guarded, and out one night only'. His coaches ran six days a week; on Sundays, Tuesdays and Thursdays they ran via Buxton, and on Monday, Wednesday and Friday via Macclesfield and Leek. There was no Saturday service.

By 1810 the General Coach Office on Great Bridgewater Street, Manchester, was advertising two direct Royal Mail coaches to London per day (departing at 1.30 p.m.), as well as services to Glasgow via Bolton, Preston, Lancaster and Carlisle to Edinburgh via Carlisle, to Birmingham via Worcester and to York, Hull, and Newcastle via Rochdale, Halifax and Leeds. Bowling, Willan & Co. of Leeds began running coaches daily to London, departing Leeds at 9 p.m., travelling overnight, and arriving in London at 5 a.m. 'from whence it returns, every Evening at Eight o'clock'. They also ran a coach to Liverpool, departing Leeds at 3 a.m., with a coach leaving for Sheffield at the same time, where it met onward coaches to Derby, Birmingham and Bristol.

Road coaches were prodigious users of horses. The *Berkshire Chronicle* estimated in summer 1835 that for the 187 miles from London to Manchester, 'the number of horses employed ... is nearly 200', and that, 'on an average, these horses annually consume 700 acres of land'.

Nor was coaching without its risks. In March 1838 (the year of our journey), the *Peveril* coach between Manchester and London collided with a farmer's cart at Hotsandwell Bridge 'in consequence of the darkness of the night, and the bad state of the roads'. The front part of the coach was ripped off and the horses were separated from the vehicle and galloped off, still in their harnesses. On the same day, a Birmingham to London coach overturned in a Coventry

Often romanticised in Christmas cards, stagecoach travel involved long journeys over indifferent roads in cold or wet weather.

street when the horses were spooked and again went 'galloping off at full speed', spilling off the outside passengers and luggage. One early railway traveller, writing to a Sheffield newspaper in October 1830, opined that:

> Who is there of age twenty-one and upwards, that has not been overturned or nearly overturned, when travelling by coach? For my part I have been twice upset, and a thousand times in imminent danger of it ... the degree of danger in travelling on a turnpike road by the mail, or a stagecoach, is ten times as great as on the ... railway.

The railways had a major advantage over the coaches in that coaches were heavily taxed until 1842. Thus, not only were the coaches slower, and more expensive, they could never hope to compete with the railways as a business. Under competition from the railways, many coach operators cut their prices drastically, barely breaking even. Unlike the canal companies, the road lobby didn't waste money fighting the railways in costly court or Parliamentary business, and instead adapted, providing connecting or 'branch coaches' feeding in to the railways. At Warrington, on the Warrington & Newton Railway, for example, mail coaches and stagecoaches were loaded on to open 'carriage wagons' for onward travel by rail to Liverpool or Manchester. This was a tradition continued by the Grand Junction Railway, which incorporated the W&N following William Chapman & Co. of The Swan with Two Necks, in Lad Lane, London, advertised the following from July 1837:

> ROYAL MAILS and FAST COACHES to BIRMINGHAM,
> connecting with the
> GRAND JUNCTION RAILWAY to:
> MANCHESTER
> LIVERPOOL, and
> SCOTLAND
> At SEVEN, EIGHT, NINE and TEN, Mornings
> At Five, Six, Seven, Eight and Nine, Evenings

From Birmingham Curzon Street, the coaches continued their onward journey by rail, rather like a modern Eurostar, with a roll-on/roll-off service.

Travelling by one's own private coach on the railway was a tradition that lasted well into the nineteenth century. The Duke of Wellington is known to have preferred this mode of travel, and the last recorded person doing so was Mrs Caroline Prodgers (d. 1890) in the 1880s. One enterprising coach proprietor, Charles Lacy of Manchester, designed and built the first road-rail vehicle, which could be run on road wheels to the railhead, and then be lowered on to a set of railway wheels for its onward journey:

> This vehicle has been constructed so that it may be drawn upon its own wheels from the residence of any Gentleman to the railway, and the body of the carriage may then be raised from the wheels by means of a crane and placed upon a frame or wagon having wheels adapted for the railway. It is then conveyed along the line and at the end of the journey may be replaced upon a set of ordinary wheels and driven along the streets to the final destination of the passenger or family, for whose exclusive use it may be devoted ... It is elegantly fitted up and is capable of containing six individuals inside and two in front ... The present carriage has been ordered merely by way of Experiment and it is not yet certain whether this novel mode of conveyance will be finally adopted.

The opening of railways was an impetus to increase short-distance coach traffic: one coach proprietor in Bradford started running the 'Railway Coach' from Bradford to Leeds from May 1835, 'to run during the season ... from the Sun Inn, Bradford, direct to the Leeds & Selby Railway depot', from whence passengers would be conveyed by train to Selby and then by

Perhaps the ultimate in luxury travel was going by your own private coach, carried by a special 'carriage truck' – a fashion the Duke of Wellington preferred, and which only died out in the 1880s.

Charles Lacy of Manchester designed and constructed this 'road-rail' carriage, which could be lifted off its road wheels, on to railway wheels, and back again.

*4*

coach to fashionable destinations on the east coast. Messrs. Bromley & Lees of Blackburn started running a coach from Blackburn to Bolton 'every morning except Sundays', which left Blackburn at 6 a.m. and arrived at the Railway Office, Bolton, in time for the 'half-past eight train for Liverpool [via Manchester]', with a connection on the return leg at 5 p.m. This made it possible to travel from Blackburn to Liverpool and back in one day, which would have been a real boon for business travellers.

Other coach owners took advantage of the fact that the London–Manchester route had a considerable (17 miles) detour, and from the opening of the Grand Junction Railway to Crewe, Messrs. Linley, Jones & Livesley of Macclesfield commenced running a coach to Manchester from Crewe via Macclesfield, providing a direct link to Manchester. The coaches ran six days a week, departing from Macclesfield at 6 a.m. and arriving at Crewe 'in time for the trains leaving Birmingham at 6 and Liverpool at half-past 6[a.m.]'. Thomas Wadell & Co. of Birmingham ran a competing coach service from Birmingham and Crewe to Manchester via Stockport and the Potteries, departing Birmingham at 12 noon and arriving in Manchester at 9.30 p.m., commencing in the summer of 1837. It was only in 1842, and after much jockeying for position, that the Manchester & Birmingham Railway, which ran direct from Manchester to Crewe, provided a cut off, in much the same way as the earlier road coaches had done.

In September 1838, the London & Birmingham opened throughout, which meant that our prospective northern traveller wishing to visit London on business or pleasure now had a third travelling option: making the journey by train.

## The Railway Station

Britain's two earliest purpose-built railway stations were at Crown Street, Liverpool, and Liverpool Road, Manchester. It was from these two terminal stations – then termed 'Coaching Offices' – that tickets could be purchased for train travel, and trains could be boarded and alighted from. Liverpool Road occupies a cramped site on what was then the edge of town, on an escarpment leading down to the River Irwell. Its architecture is dignified neo-Grecian – the main façade being rendered with fashionable stucco. Here were separate first- and second-class booking halls and a goods office.

Separate provision of booking and waiting space for first- and second-class passengers followed coaching practice. It would be anachronistic to suppose that the separate booking areas and waiting areas solely reflected the social hierarchy, and that first class equated with the socially superior, and second class with the socially inferior. Rather, there was a practical distinction. The first class represented a 'direct' or non-stop service, equating with the mail coach, while second class was the 'stopper', and equivalent to the slower stagecoach (although even the second-class rail service typically stopped only by request). It made sense to segregate passengers waiting for the different *types* of trains. By the late 1830s this had begun to change, with the introduction of 'mixed' trains carrying both first- and second-class passengers in their respective carriages.

At Liverpool Road, the rail level was at first-floor height, and one passenger remarked that in ascending the staircase to their rail-level waiting room they were entering a different world, and leaving the hustle and bustle of street life (and therefore the road) behind:

> There is something singularly striking, and, to a contemplative mind, instructive, in this sudden change in our altitude – this alteration in our relative position to our fellow men. But a moment ago we were in the midst, and made a little part, of a busy multitude ... anon we find ourselves, as it were ... translated to another equally sublunary scene, from which we discern the self-same beings of our previous companionship ... in a world that now lies stretched far beneath us.

Liverpool Road station, Manchester, was built in phases by David Bellhouse Junior of Manchester between 1830 and 1831.

The spacious first-class booking office at Liverpool Road, for those passengers wishing to travel non-stop between Liverpool and Manchester.

The graceful curving staircase connecting the first-class booking office to the first-class waiting room above – access to which was for ticket-holders only.

The rail-level façade of Liverpool Road *c.* 1900: the first-class exit is on the right, and the second-class exit is on the left. The lack of any raised platform meant passengers had to physically climb into their carriages – exactly as they had to do with stagecoaches.

The same view over a century later, following the restoration of Liverpool Road to become the home of the Museum of Science & Industry, Manchester.

Passengers and passengers alone would have remained in the well-appointed waiting rooms until the bell was rung, calling them to their train five minutes before it was to depart; hence the lack of accommodation at rail level – there was no need for passengers to wait on the platform, it was merely a space to be crossed before climbing into your compartment while the porters manhandled your luggage onto the roof. It would have been noisy, hectic and dangerous, as both arriving and departing trains made use of the same passenger buildings, which must have presented additional overcrowding at busy times.

It was only in 1837, with the arrival of the Grand Junction Railway, that a separate 'arrivals station' was built, with Liverpool Road becoming the 'departure station.' The arrivals station was approached on its south side by a long ramp from Water Street for pedestrians and a carriage ramp on the north side. It boasted an overall roof supported on iron columns. Underneath it were stables, mess rooms and kitchens for railway personnel.

Crown Street appears to have been better planned as it was passenger-only (goods traffic being segregated to Wapping). There were separate first- and second-class booking halls and waiting rooms, but this time at rail level. The station was again single-sided with departing and arriving trains pulling up alongside the handsome coaching office. There was a raised kerb – not quite a platform proper – and passengers and rolling stock were protected from the elements by an overall roof, which covered three tracks. T. T. Bury's famous print implies that there might have been a departure and arrival side, with a carriage road down the middle. Thus, it is probably Crown Street that marks the start of the railway station as its own distinct architectural tradition, rather than Liverpool Road.

The next development of the railway station was Marsh Lane, Leeds, on the Leeds & Selby (opened 1834), which had a triple-span overall roof that covered four 'lines of way.' As at Liverpool Road, the booking offices were on the ground floor and the station itself was elevated at first-floor level, approached by a 'spacious staircase'. The station was divided

The 'arrivals station' at Liverpool Road opened in December 1837 and was where trains from Liverpool set down their passengers. Travellers to Liverpool still caught their train from Liverpool Road. The impressive triumphal arch housed the water tank for the locomotives.

Crown Street station, Liverpool, was recognisably a railway station, with an overall roof, raised platforms and the segregation of goods and passengers.

into arrival and departure sides (a considerable improvement from Liverpool Road), but, as at Liverpool Road, no platforms were provided and goods were not segregated from passengers:

> There is, however, no platform on either side, so that the passengers are obliged to mount the carriages by the carriage-steps, which is attended by considerable inconvenience, especially to ladies ... there are commodious warehouses; and a new one has lately been erected for the purpose of keeping the passenger-shed free from the mixed business which has hitherto been carried on in it.

Liverpool Road would have been quaint and old-fashioned compared to the newly built Liverpool Lime Street, Birmingham Curzon Street or London Euston. Indeed, John Herapath, founder and editor of *The Railway Magazine*, thought the whole line looked half finished, 'reflecting the features, not of a rich and flourishing company, but of abject pitiable poverty'.

Philip Hardwick's grand entrance to Curzon Street station, Birmingham, which was opened in 1838 for the Grand Junction and London & Birmingham railways.

The train shed at Curzon Street. The departure platform faces the booking offices and the waiting rooms are on the right. Arrivals are on the left, separated by carriage sidings.

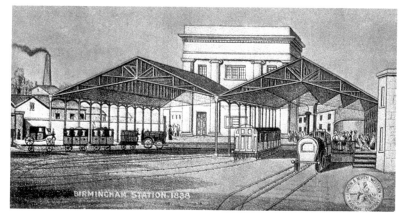

Euston Square station, London & Birmingham Railway, in 1838. The departure platform is on the left and the arrivals platform is on the right, which is once again separated by carriage sidings.

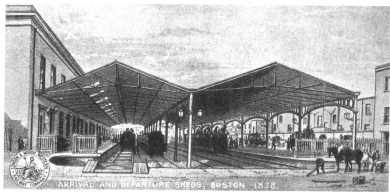

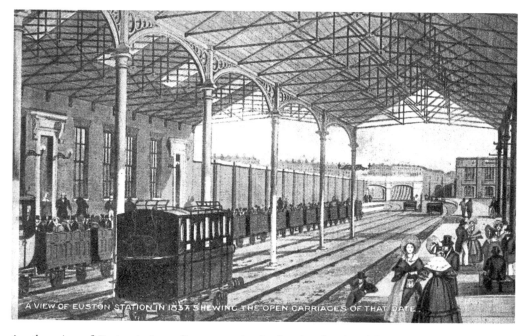

Another view of Euston in its earliest years. A mixed train of enclosed first and open 'day seconds' stands at the departure platform, while an enclosed 'night second' stands in one of the carriage sidings.

These three later stations show how rapid the development of the railway station, and the maturity of its architecture, had been. Liverpool Road looked back to the coaching tradition, while Euston *et al* had all the features identifiable with a railway station in the twenty-first century, including raised platforms and overall roofs.

At Lime Street, Francis Wishaw described how:

> There are two carriage gateways for the arrival and departure of common-road carriages; the arrival gateway being on the left, and the departure gateway on the right of the railway.
>
> There are four lines of way at the station ... the whole being covered with light roofing, supported on cast iron columns. The booking office of the Company, and those of the Grand Junction Company are contiguous to each other, and are on the left side of the railway.

Passengers entered the station through the arched gateway on the left, where the booking offices, waiting room and departure platforms were. Trains arrived into the arrival platform on the right-hand side, and passengers departed through the right-hand (when viewed from the street) gateway. Between the two platforms were carriage sidings – all four being connected via eleven turntables, so that carriages could be uncoupled, turned and shunted around the station by hand. The main façade into Lime Street was 330 feet in length, was built from 'white freestone', and was 'decorated by thirty-six three-quarter columns of the Corinthian order ... surmounted by a chaste and beautiful entablature'. The building cost over £6,000, with £2,000 being given by Liverpool Corporation.

> Behind the left centre of the façade, are the forwarding and booking offices of the Liverpool & Manchester and Grand Junction Companies, for both passengers and parcels. These offices open into the station-yard opposite to where trains start. The compartment

The main façade of Liverpool Lime Street, which was opened by the Liverpool & Manchester Railway in 1836 and partially financed by Liverpool Corporation.

of the building on the left ... contains the general offices of the Grand Junction Company, while those on the opposite side of the left-hand archway, are the general offices of the Liverpool & Manchester Company ... the extensive buildings on the left side of the grand area are the workshops of the Liverpool & Manchester Company. Here are coachmakers', smiths', painters and all other description of workshops, necessary for the complete manufacture of carriages used on the line. The opposite side of the area is entirely occupied by the workshops of the Grand Junction Company.

The overall roof was 70 feet wide and was a 'work of admirable skill', supported on arches and columns of cast iron. The raised platforms were termed 'landing wharfs'.

Curzon Street in Birmingham, jointly operated by the Grand Junction and London & Birmingham, presented a handsome Ionic frontage with the train shed behind. The train shed roof was in two spans of 58 feet, and was 233 feet long. Wishaw proudly announced that, 'The ... platforms are 20 feet in width, and on a level with the floors of the carriages.' As at Lime Street, there were arrival and departure platforms, which were separated by carriage sidings. Euston was of a similar plan but, despite its grand and imposing buildings by Hardwick, the station area itself was smaller than at Curzon Street: only 80 feet by 200, with two platforms and four running roads – the middle two being carriage sidings.

Euston and Lime Street also shared the fact that no locomotive entered them in their first few decades; rather, trains were worked down into both stations by stationary engines. At Liverpool, the town fathers, although voting several thousand pounds for the new station, forbade the entrance of locomotives within town limits. Thus, all trains were worked by cable until the 1880s. The use of rope-worked trains at Euston was also due to 'NIMBYism', so the company's Act forbade locomotives working nearer to London than Camden.

The engine house at Camden, London & Birmingham Railway. Locomotives were not allowed to work into Euston, and so were coupled and uncoupled at Camden, with the train then being worked by stationary engine.

# Tickets Please!

For passengers arriving at the Liverpool Road station in Manchester to book their ticket for London, not only the buildings but the method of purchasing a ticket would have been familiar to any who had travelled by road coach. On the Liverpool & Manchester, tickets could be purchased at either of the two terminal stations (Liverpool Road or Lime Street), or from the company offices on Market Street in Manchester or Dale Street in Liverpool. A connecting road omnibus service was briefly provided from the offices to the station for first-class passengers, picking them up at certain points en route.

Initially, tickets had to be purchased twenty-four hours in advance, and the traveller had to provide their name, age, address, details of why they wished to travel, as well as details of next of kin – exactly as they would have done when booking a seat on a stage- or mail coach. As with road travelling, the company did not hold itself responsible for any damage to persons or their luggage during the journey. Printed on the back were extracts from the company's by-laws reminding passengers not to smoke or consume alcohol in the carriages or on the company's property, that it was not lawful to pay any of the company servants a tip, and (from 1833) to remain seated in case of emergency. Subsequently, they could be purchased up to half an hour before departure, at which point the booking office doors were closed and locked.

Tickets on the Liverpool & Manchester measured 4¼ inches by 1½ inches, with counterfoils of the same size. They were completed by hand and details were entered into the waybill book (hence the term 'booking'), assigning each passenger a specific seat in a specific carriage for a train at a set time. In an early attempt to prevent fraud ('revenue protection', in modern parlance), the London & Birmingham tickets were 'of different colours for Up and Down, and for each class of carriage'. Each booking clerk kept a diagram with the number of coaches, which were named or numbered, and seat numbers to which a corresponding number for each ticket sold was issued. Once in possession of a ticket, it not only granted the holder to a seat on the train, but it also allowed them entry to the outer waiting room at rail level. One traveller in October 1830 recounted:

> Each passenger has a numbered ticket delivered to him when the place is paid for. The seats are also numbered, and this ensures him that seat in the carriage by which he intends to travel, bearing its allotted numeral. [In second-class] the seats are also numbered, but you are not compelled to take the same number as is borne on your ticket. The old rule is observed, 'first come, first served', and he that comes last has only 'Hobson's choice'.

If the train was missed, only a 50 per cent refund was available if the passenger presented their ticket within forty-eight hours and there weren't any refunds at all in case of lateness or cancellation. The Liverpool & Manchester did not guarantee that any train would run as advertised, nor would it guarantee that the trains ran to time, or ran at all.

Not everyone was impressed with queuing for hand-written tickets. One correspondent to *The Polytechnic Journal* in November 1839 fumed that:

> Many blanks have to be filled up in the tickets while the public are crowding round to obtain them. Surely all this formality or scribbling is not necessary? Why not have all the tickets for the day ready for delivery, or in some condition of readiness so as to require as little writing and delay as possible?

Any discrepancy between tickets sold and fares collected was to be taken from the pay of the booking clerks. As a result, they, and others who handled money, had to find sureties ranging from £100 to £200. The chief clerk at Liverpool Road was discharged in 1833 after two guards reported him for entering less 'road money' (fares collected along the line) than they had brought in; one assistant ticket clerk managed to gamble away £170 of the company's money, and on Christmas Eve 1833 at Crown Street, the day's takings (£57 in coin) were stolen from

*Left*: A busy mid-Victorian depiction of the railway station; a railway constable is prominent in his top hat, which remained part of their uniform for most of the nineteenth century.

*Right*: Dignity personified! An LNWR passenger guard in all his splendour, *c.* 1850. Dark green tunic and cap, with silver Russia braid and elaborate cartouche pouch.

the safe. Chief Clerk John Kyle's usual practice was to take the locked tin containing the day's takings home with him so that it was not left in the office overnight, but on that particular evening he had left his wife to lock up and she had left the tin in the safe. It was only when he found the need to enter the safe on the afternoon of Christmas Day that Kyle discovered the takings were missing. He was admonished by the Board for failing to take the money home with him that night. As a result, fireproof iron Chubb safes were installed at Crown Street and Liverpool Road.

The station superintendent, his assistant and team of clerks were to ensure that no passenger was admitted to the trains, or exited the station, without displaying their 'proper ticket':

> Taking care that no person is admitted inside the inclosure [i.e. on the platform] till the train stops at the station, and the porters assist the guards in placing the passengers in the proper carriages ... From the time of arrival to that of departure, the trains are to be under his [i.e. the inspector's] direction...
>
> No person must be allowed to pass by ... without first producing a ticket; and any person arriving by a train at any station without such ticket, must pay the fare from the place when the train originally started.

Before passengers were allowed to board the train, or exit a station, the guard was to:

> Examine the tickets of all persons in first- and second-class carriages and pay particular attention to the date and station printed on each ticket ... [and] that passengers get into the proper class of carriage.

19

On the LNWR – successor to the London & Birmingham, Grand Junction and Liverpool & Manchester – the guards and station clerks were to ensure that:

No person is to be allowed to pass on the platform without producing his ticket.

If the Guard or Station Clerk have reason to suspect that any Passenger is or has been travelling upon the Railway without having paid any Fare or the proper Fare, he may require such person to produce his Ticket; and every Passenger before leaving the Company's premises at the end of his journey is to be required to deliver up his Ticket. If any passenger shall refuse or be unable to produce a proper Ticket, or shall commit any other offence ... the case shall be immediately investigated by the Chief Clerk of the Station where the occurrence may take place ...

Passengers not producing their Tickets are to be required to deposit the amount of the Whole Fare from the place whence the Train started until the inquiry can be made, in order to ascertain whether the Fare has been actually paid or not, and in every case the circumstances must be inquired into without delay ...

The power of detention is to be exercised with great caution, and never where the address of the party is known, or adequate security offered for his appearance to answer the charge. When it shall be found necessary to detain any party, such detention shall not continue for a longer period than is absolutely necessary, but he shall be conveyed before a Magistrate with as little delay as possible.

The LNWR gave the benefit of doubt to those passengers who 'travell[ed] beyond the distance for which they have paid their Fare unintentionally, or even against their wish'. Fines and detention were reserved for those who 'wilfully proceed beyond the place to which they are booked', and those who travelled without a ticket 'with intent to avoid payment thereof'. Railway constables and guards had the power of arrest and on the Grand Junction Railway in November 1838, 'a person named Donelly' was brought before the local magistrates. Donelly had booked a place on the train from Stafford to Warrington, but on arrival 'refused to alight, and insisted upon being conveyed to Liverpool'. He then 'violently remonstrated' with the guard and conductor and at Liverpool 'was given over into custody', before being sent before the county magistrate and fined 40s. Another Grand Junction passenger was arrested, sent before the bench, and fined for smoking on the platform at Newton Junction.

Struggling with heavy bags, being hemmed in on all sides and having little space to manoeuvre often led to tempers fraying:

The method of herding and driving passengers is unbecoming, offensive and not necessary. There is generally a passage between the [ticket] counter on one side and the rails on the other, and passengers have to huddle through like going into the pit of a theatre on a crowded night. The passengers are squeezed. It is impossible to carry much luggage ... and if you set it down behind you in the waiting-room for the porters, it may be lost; or if you personally give it to a porter, you do not know whereabouts he may deposit it, which will be most particularly awkward.

Initially only available to first-class passengers on the Liverpool & Manchester, porters were readily identifiable through their wearing of olive green jackets and caps, white fustian trousers and a brass plaque on each arm bearing their company's heraldic arms and the porter's individual number. Porters received new clothing twice a year (April and October) and 1s per week for six months was to be deducted from their pay to cover the cost of their uniforms. Any porter found accepting a gratuity – a common practice on stagecoaches, and indeed there must have been great temptation to accept one given the low pay (20s per week) and long hours – was to be dismissed from service, even in the case of one porter who ran through the Crown Street tunnel to retrieve a hat box that had fallen from a train for a passenger, and was seen to receive a gratuity by way of thanks. Goods porters wore brown jackets and caps. Coach and luggage porters and guards were compelled to wear their brass arm-badges under the threat of a 1s fine. When it was found that porters were not wearing their badges, the Board ordered that they be sewn to their clothes (1839).

## Timetabling

Timetables would have been unfamiliar to early railway companies. Lines such as the Liverpool & Manchester followed stagecoach practice by publishing departure times in newspapers and on bill posters, but never arrival. Enterprising publishers such as James Cornish of London produced printed 'Railway Companions', but it was the Manchester Quaker, engraver and mapmaker George Bradshaw who first published his 'Time Table' on 19 October 1839, entitled *Bradshaw's Railway Time Tables and Assistant to Railway Travelling*, thus introducing the timetable as we now know it.

Then, as now, the railway system was fragmented, and run by different companies. For example, the journey from Liverpool or Manchester to London involved three companies. For passengers to the south from Liverpool or Manchester, six trains departed from either terminal station to Birmingham via Newton Junction on the Liverpool & Manchester. Only the 8.30 a.m. and 4.30 p.m. trains were second class, which took upwards of six hours between the termini. The first-class train took only four and a half hours: the 6.30 a.m., arriving into Birmingham at 11.05 a.m., which enabled the first-class passenger to connect with the 12 noon departure for London, with sufficient time to stretch their legs and get something to eat. For a second-class passenger from Manchester, arriving in Birmingham at 2.00 p.m., they would have had a three-hour wait for their onward connection.

The London & Birmingham ran six trains, which connected with the Grand Junction:

| | |
|---|---|
| 8.45 a.m. | Mail |
| 12 noon | Mixed |
| 1.15 p.m. | Mixed |
| 4.00 p.m. | First |
| 5.00 p.m. | Mixed |
| 12 midnight | Mail |

'Waiting for the Train':
A rather bored-looking
passenger as depicted by the
artist of *The Illustrated London
News*.

WAITING FOR THE TRAIN.

The mixed trains stopped at all stations and were the only trains available for the second-class passenger making their way north or south. At the end of 1839, a group of 'respectable gentlemen' organised an unsuccessful petition to attach a second-class coach to every mail train on the London & Birmingham.

Not everyone was impressed with the treatment of second-class passengers; one exasperated traveller on the Grand Junction Railway wrote to the *Staffordshire Advertiser*:

> Having lately had much occasion to travel by the carriages of the Grand Junction Railway, and having suffered much inconvenience from some of their regulations ... It seems to me hard that no second-class carriages should be attached to the first-class trains, in order to enable a poor man to choose which carriage he will sit in. As it is at present, the second-class passenger has no chance of leaving Liverpool or Birmingham except at 6 o'clock a.m. or 4 o'clock p.m. – leaving a space in the heart of the day ... during which he has no means of proceeding on his journey ... the fares for the first-class passengers are so exorbitant that it is difficult for a man of slender means to avail himself of an alternative [to second-class].

## A Matter of Class

The idea of 'class' as an indicator of socio-economic status is a product of the later nineteenth century. By 1900, Britain was ordered as never before, and consciously so, into a hierarchy of classes in the Marxist and economic sense. First, second and third class were clearly marked social zones, from the clothes one wore, to how one spoke and how one travelled. In the twenty-first century, in the more meritocratic world of 'standard class' (as second-class was re-designated in 1987), 'first class' refers to a superior type of accommodation for which the traveller pays a higher fare, providing more comfortable seats, seclusion (or at least less noise), complimentary coffee, croissants and a newspaper. During the 1830s, it was customary to talk about social hierarchy or difference in terms of title, rank, or degree, rather than of class, and usually not in economic regard. It has been argued that the strict division of first, second and third class on the railway helped to establish in a broad social sense the whole concept of class in terms of socio-economic status. When catching a train in 1838, first class, and indeed the whole notion of class, was thus not only different, but also far more complicated.

First-class passengers patiently boarding their coupé-ended carriage for the Epsom Races, *c.* 1840, as depicted by *The Illustrated London News*.

Second-class passengers struggling to find the best seats for their journey to the races. *The Illustrated London News.*

A group of third-class passengers, depicted travelling by 'open boxes' to Epsom. It is interesting that the artist has depicted several persons of colour – was there racial as well as class segregation?

It was all to do with stagecoaches and mail coaches, and their terminology. The system of Royal Mail coaches was instituted in 1784. In addition to the mail, a mail coach carried a small number of inside passengers, usually first class or non-stop (other than to change horses and for an overnight stop where the journey required it). This was an exclusive, luxury way to travel. The stagecoach (so-called because they stopped at various 'stages' to change horses and allow passengers time for rest and refreshment) usually carried six passengers inside and about a dozen perched on the roof with the coachman and guard.

Due to the thirty-six bridges that crossed their railway, and the tunnel at Crown Street, the Liverpool & Manchester Railway directors forbade the travelling of passengers on the roof of carriages. This, therefore, presented a challenge to the traditional mode of travelling. The Liverpool & Manchester took the opportunity to build entire vehicles to different standards, separating the inside and outside passengers with 'close coaches' and the roofless 'blue boxes.' Thus, entire trains could be run for inside and outside passengers.

The next logical step was to run trains emulating the stagecoach and mail coach practice, with non-stop first-class trains running from Liverpool to Manchester (and vice versa), pausing only midway at Parkside to take on coke and water, as well as second-class trains, which stopped at intermediate stations by request only. In fact, as late as August 1830 the directors were proposing the changing of engines at Parkside, rather than refuelling them, as if they were changing horses on a road coach.

The March 1831 timetable from the Liverpool & Manchester indicates that both the enclosed and open coaches were used on second-class trains, and that, furthermore, both first- and second-class tickets could be had for the intermediate stations. In other words, one could travel in one of the yellow 'glass coaches' on the stopping train – the glass coaches providing inside accommodation that wasn't specifically first class.

That first and second class was more to do with speed than accommodation is made clear in the timetable of June 1838:

| By first-class train, | four inside, | Royal Mail Coach | 6s 6d |
| By first-class train, | six inside, | Glass Coach | 6s |
| By first-class train, | six inside, | Curtain Coach | 6s |
| By second-class train, | six inside, | Glass Coach | 6s |
| By second-class train, | | Open Carriages | 4s 6d |

In other words, there were three levels of first class: i.e. express accommodation by the mail coach, which sat four per compartment (initially at an extra cost of 1s); by glass coach, which sat six per compartment; and by the semi-open 'curtain coach'. These carriages, for those passengers who wished to travel in first class comfort and speed, but still get a good lungful of fresh air, had a glazed central compartment, but the two end compartments were unglazed, with leather curtains that could be drawn in case of rain.

The most comfortable way to travel by railway was by the Royal Mail coach: the compartments only sat four and could be converted into a day bed. Note the mail box carried on the roof.

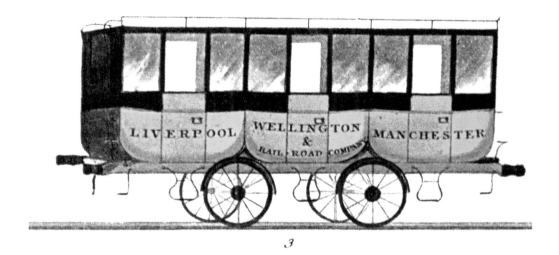

*3*

An early iron-framed Liverpool & Manchester coach with inside bearings, putting the wheels outside the body (stagecoach fashion) rather than under it, as with later designs.

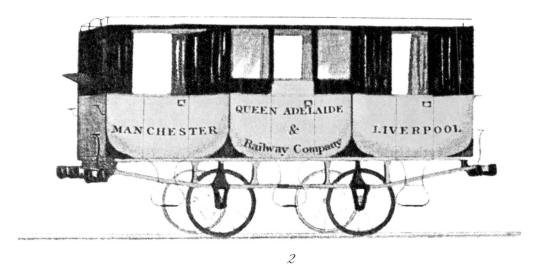

*2*

*Queen Adelaide*, one of the 'curtain coaches' for first-class travellers. The centre compartment was glazed while the windows of the end compartments could be closed by leather curtains.

Turning to the second-class trains, there were two levels of accommodation: the enclosed glass coaches seating six per compartment, or the 'open carriages', with each compartment seating eight.

The Liverpool & Manchester had also experimented with 'merchant's trains' in 1836. These were mixed accommodation, with three first-class and three second-class coaches, and ran at first-class speed – departing from either end of the line at 7.00 p.m. and pausing only to take on water.

A well-known depiction of a Liverpool & Manchester 'blue box', or second-class coach, by Ackerman. These were described by contemporaries as resembling a set of church pews on wheels.

Another type of early Liverpool & Manchester second-class coach had passengers seated on longitudinal (rather than transverse) benches.

Not only were two types of train in operation, but two types of station also. There were first-class stations, where every train stopped and had refreshment rooms for first-class ticket holders, and second-class stations, or 'stopping' stations, which were request stops – hence the passenger having to book their ticket in advance so that if they wished to be set down at a second-class station, that information could be collected and handed to the guards and driver so that they knew where they had to stop.

A paper is given to each engine-driver upon his departure with a train, on which is noted down his own name and the name of the fire-man, the name of the engine, the time of starting, and the number of coaches, [carriage] trucks, and laden wagons with which his train is made up, and any special instructions for the purposes of traffic.

If a passenger wished to catch a train from a second-class station, a blue flag or signal board was displayed, informing the oncoming train to stop 'for purposes of traffic'. Only the first-class stations were timetabled and had scheduled stops. Second-class stations were by request only. Of this system, Henry Booth, General Manager of the Liverpool & Manchester, said in 1841:

We have twenty stopping places ... we do not stop at all places, but we sometimes stop at six or eight on half the line [the Liverpool end], and scarcely have stoppages on the other half; on the other half, we make up for the delay on the other half ... but if we were to be limited by a time-table, we must be stopping at every one of the 20 stations, which would delay us quarter of an hour.

Booth noted there was a 'considerable ... loss of time' caused through stopping en route, and that drivers were urged to make up lost time by fast running, often going as quickly as 30 mph

A first-class train halted at the first-class station at Newton, where first-class passengers could avail themselves of refreshments courtesy of the Leigh Arms Hotel.

between stations. First-class trains were timed to take ninety minutes and second-class would take two hours, with the latter, in fact, having a higher line speed between stops.

On the Grand Junction, it was only in first-class trains that a seat could be booked; seats in the mixed trains were on a first-come, first-served basis. The Grand Junction referred to second-class stations as 'road stations' and said of prospective passengers joining the trains:

> [They] are desired to be in good time, as the train will leave each station when ready, the main object being to perform the whole journey as expeditiously as possible. Passengers will be book[ed] only conditionally, upon there being room upon arrival of the trains, and they will have a preference of seats in the order in which they are booked.

## Conditions of Carriage

Many early railway companies stipulated their 'Conditions of Carriage' in their by-laws, which were gained as part of their Act. The railway constables – all sworn-in special constables – had the powers of arrest for any person breaking these by-laws on railway property. The Liverpool & Manchester forbade the drinking of alcohol and smoking (which was then, as now, viewed as an unhealthy public nuisance):

> Even with the general consent of the Passengers present, as the annoyance will be experienced in a still greater degree by those who may occupy the same coach on the succeeding journey.

Despite warnings to not smoke being printed on the backs of tickets, first-class passengers obviously continued to do so. By 1835 the directors had had enough and ordered printed signs to be pasted in every carriage reminding passengers of the prohibition against smoking. These notices had little effect; the Rev. William Gaskell, Minister of Cross Street Unitarian Chapel in Manchester, was of the opinion that the provision of smoking-only carriages would end the 'nuisance' to other passengers, especially to females. That said, Gaskell was an ardent teetotaller, who also believed public smoking to be a nuisance and 'dangerous to the health' generally. The Liverpool & Manchester directors eventually drew up a by-law banning the consumption of tobacco on railway property, under a fine of £2.

The sale of food and drink (especially alcohol) by platform vendors to passengers resulted in another by-law of 1837, forbidding the sale of any food, drink or intoxicating substance on railway property. Unusually, Eccles cakes were singled out – presumably because they had an alcohol content at this period. Hungry passengers, however, soon began to pester the directors for the return of refreshment vendors at stations. So too did local tavern owners, even threatening legal action, but the directors stood firm. If a passenger felt that they could not make the two-hour trip (second class) between Liverpool and Manchester without refreshment, then they were at liberty to bring their own. Relief of the other sort was an entirely different matter, as there were no public lavatories on any train or at any station.

The Grand Junction Railway resolved that:

> No person will be allowed to sell liquors or eatables of any kind upon the line. The Company earnestly hope that the Public will co-operate with them in enforcing this regulation, as it will be the means of removing a cause of delay, and greatly diminish the chance of an accident.

Passengers arriving at Liverpool Road could avail themselves of a meal and a comfortable bed courtesy of Benjamin Taylor, who opened the Railway & Commercial Inn opposite the new station in September 1830:

GOOD REASONS.

*Punch Magazine*'s take on the issue of railway smoking:

Railway Official: 'You'd better *not* smoke, sir.'
Passenger: 'That's what my friends say.'
Railway Official: 'But you *mustn't* smoke, sir.'
Passenger: 'So my Doctor tells me.'
Railway Official: 'But you *shan't* smoke, Sir!'
Passenger: 'So my wife tells me.'

> He has OPENED a NEW and COMMODIOUS INN, immediately opposite the Company's
> Offices, where BREAKFASTS, DINNERS &c. are regularly provided for the accommodation of
> such Passengers, at times suitable for the arrival and departure of the conveyances.

The Railway and Commercial Inn also advertised 'private apartments, [and] spacious and well-aired bedrooms', with an 'airy situation, in country part of town'. They also advertised 'breakfasts, chops, steaks, or dinners on the shortest notice' to railway passengers, as well as 'good stabling with lock-ups and coach houses'.

The practice of the Liverpool & Manchester running omnibuses for their passengers was soon discontinued due to the number of trains being delayed as the buses were late. In order to encourage the bus drivers to be on time, the directors issued a regulation stating that they had to be at the station at least ten minutes before departure time.

Passengers were only allowed onto the area at rail level five minutes before the train was due to depart, when a large bell was rung to alert passengers. Friends, family and well-wishers were not allowed one final embrace as a loved one boarded the train – in fact, unless they had a ticket, they would not have even been allowed into the waiting room! Porters rang hand-bells on the platform in order to hurry up passengers. Doors to the waiting rooms were locked ten minutes 'before train time', and no person was to be admitted after that.

The by-laws of the Sheffield & Rotherham Railway (opened 1839) are typical examples of railway discipline from this period:

1. No person shall smoke Tobacco in any Carriage, or on the Line or Stations, under a Penalty not exceeding 40s, no less than 5s.
2. In Order to prevent accidents, it is Requested that Passengers do not get in or out of, or open the door of any Carriage on the off side, unless so desired by a Servant of the Company.
3. No Passenger shall ride, or be permitted to ride upon any Engine or Tender, under a Penalty not exceeding £5, nor less than 20s.
4. No Passenger shall Ride upon the Steps or Platforms of any Carriage, under a Penalty not exceeding 40s.
5. No person shall travel on the Railway, or take his seat in or on any Carriage with an intention to travel on the Railway without having first paid his Fare, and obtained a Ticket for the particular Class of Carriage in which he shall so travel or take his seat, under a Penalty of £5.
6. Passengers shall produce and deliver up their Tickets when requested by the Company's Servants, under a Penalty not exceeding 20s.
7. No person shall wilfully present, or ride with a false Ticket, in order to defraud the company, under a Penalty not exceeding £5.
8. Passengers at the Intermediate Stations will be considered as taking their Tickets conditionally only; that is to say, in case there shall be room in the passenger Train.
9. Persons being intoxicated shall go off the Line and Stations on being required to do so by any Servant of the Company, or they will be removed by Force.
10. Passengers shall not remain on the Stations longer than necessary to leave the Trains and in to receive their luggage, but shall afterwards leave the Station on being required by any Servant of the Company.

The company also reserved the right to remove or even arrest persons for foul language, disorderly conduct and vandalism:

11. Persons writing or using abusive, profane, or obscene words or language, or being disorderly, or making a disturbance, or annoying the Passengers on the Line or Stations, or in the Carriage, or obstructing or resisting any of the Company's Officers and Servants in the exercise of their Duty, will be removed from the Company's Premises, and shall forfeit their Fare, and pay a Penalty not exceeding £3.
12. Any passenger Cutting or Damaging any Carriage, or the Lining thereof, or breaking the windows thereof, shall make good the damage, or in default shall pay a Penalty not exceeding £5 nor less than 40s.

Members of the public found trespassing on the railway or interfering with the points, 'switches or sidings of the railway' were subject to a £5 fine and would be removed from company property by one of the railway constables.

# CHAPTER 2

# The Railway Carriage

The first purpose-built railway carriage was the *Experiment*, which was designed by George Stephenson for the Stockton & Darlington Railway. The vehicle was double-ended (so as to avoid the need to turn it at journey's end) and was horse-drawn. It resembled nothing more than a garden shed fitted with longitudinal benches along each side. The S&D began carrying passengers in October 1825, and *Experiment* ran four return trips per week at a cost of 1s, taking two hours to cover the 12 or so miles from Stockton to Darlington. A second coach, the *Express*, began running in April 1826: while *Experiment* resembled a garden shed, *Express* consisted of a stagecoach body on a wooden underframe, which carried four iron railway wheels. It too was double-ended, and carried eight passengers – four inside and four outside. Another stagecoach on railway wheels named the *Union* began running in October, which, in addition to Stockton and Darlington, 'will call at Yarm, and will pass within a mile of Middleton Spa on its way'. Fares were 1s ½d inside and 1d per mile outside.

And thus, to all intents and purposes, the development of the railway carriage ended.

The world's first railway passenger coach, *Experiment*, designed by George Stephenson for the Stockton & Darlington Railway in 1825.

# Enter the Worsdells

The world's first purpose-built railway carriage manufactory was established at Crown Street, Liverpool, by Thomas Clarke Worsdell II (1788–1862) and his eldest son Nathaniel Worsdell (1809–1886). The Worsdells were members of the Religious Society of Friends (Quakers), a religious movement founded by George Fox (1624–1691). Quakers meet for religious worship in silence, and are well known for their pacifism, simplicity of living and their honest and ethical business dealing.

Thomas was introduced to George Stephenson around 1828. Stephenson called him 'the best coachmaker I ever knew' and, according to Nathaniel, in his old age:

> In 1828 ... I and my father in consultation with George Stephenson ... planned the first railway carriage. Stephenson produced a sketch of what he thought might possibly do for a railway carriage. My father and I being practical coachbuilders ... we suggested certain improvements ... the first carriage that ever travelled between Manchester and Liverpool was built from that sketch.

Thomas was appointed superintendent of the coaching department of the Liverpool & Manchester in 1828, with carriage-building facilities at Crown Street. The Worsdells had settled in Lancashire in 1827, and the excellence of their work had brought them to the attention of fellow Quaker James Cropper, one of the directors of the Liverpool & Manchester. In 1829 the Worsdells were advertising for:

> Two coach-body makers, who can have constant employ, either by the piece or day-work. Steady-men will meet with a comfortable situation.

The Worsdells were employed by the Liverpool & Manchester until 1837. Between 1829 and 1836 the company had produced all its coaching stock in-house, and had even been invited to build carriages for the Dublin & Kingstown Railway in 1834, but had to decline due to their works being fully occupied. With the closure of Crown Street in 1836 and the opening

A late Victorian print, 'The Carriage Builder'.

of Lime Street in 1837–8, the Carriage & Wagon Works were reorganised and were relocated to Lime Street in a building specially designed for the purpose. It was of two storeys, with four railway lines running directly into the ground floor. Trap doors connected the upper floor with the lower, so that components, and even complete carriage bodies, could be raised or lowered.

During this reorganisation, Thomas resigned in January 1837 to take charge of the rolling stock – and locomotives – of the fledgling Leipzig & Dresden Railway, taking his wife Sarah and his younger sons with him to live in Germany. Nathaniel also left the Liverpool & Manchester to join the Grand Junction Company (to be opened in summer 1837) as their coaching superintendent. John Pownall, who was appointed in February 1837, succeeded the Worsdells in Liverpool. Pownall had previously been a journeyman coachbuilder for Henry Whalley, a local coachmaker who recommended him to the Board.

The Liverpool & Manchester had started to outsource rolling stock production the previous year. In September 1836, the directors ordered six new first-class and one Royal Mail coach from Richard Melling of Manchester as the Board considered their works to be already overstretched and unable to complete the new carriages to the required standard by the summer of 1837, when the Grand Junction began running. It was with these second-generation coaches by Melling that many of the improvements suggested by Henry Booth were implemented, including sprung buffing gear and draw gear of his own design.

## The First Carriages

The earliest first-class carriages on the Liverpool & Manchester were based upon stagecoach designs. One contemporary account described them as:

> [Being] like French Diligences, of two or three bodies joined together ... The seats which accommodate three persons each are at least twice as wide as a four-inside stagecoach, so as to allow the same space for three as is now allotted to four. Between the sittings is a rest for the arms, and each passenger has a cushion to himself; and there is also a little projection against which he may rest his head; and the backs are padded and covered with fine cloth, like in a private carriage; so that passengers may sit and sleep with as much comfort and luxury as if he were in an easy chair or sofa. There is abundant space left for the legs. The external appearance of the coaches is nearly equal to a fine carriage. There are no outside passengers; and they carry no luggage.

> (*Chester Chronicle*, 11 June 1830)

The *Gentleman's Magazine* thought that the new first-class carriages on the Liverpool & Manchester gave 'quite a new idea of the ease and luxury with which persons may in future travel'.

In the early days of the Liverpool & Manchester, the Worsdells appear to have experimented with different forms of first-class vehicle, including one with coupé ends – that is, a half compartment at each end with large glass windows across the end wall. The Worsdells also experimented with both inside and outside bearings for the wheels, before eventually settling on outside bearings, which enabled wider bodies to be used. The *Liverpool Times* described them in June 1830:

> The Steam Carriages vary in their size and plan; some are intended to accommodate four persons in each body, and others six; and some have a central compartment which will contain six persons, with seats before and behind, and two other compartments, one in front and one in rear, each of them resembling a post-chaise, with windows in front, containing only three persons. The seats which accommodate three persons are at least as wide as a four inside stagecoach.

A Liverpool & Manchester first-class or 'close coach' depicted by Ackerman in 1831; note the guard perched on his seat and the large amounts of luggage carried on the roof.

Replica close coach *Huskisson*, built by the LMS at Derby in 1930 based on drawings taken from a model by Nathaniel Worsdell in 1838. (Lauren Jaye Gradwell)

Another view of *Huskisson* showing details of the buffing gear, steps and the guard's seat. (Matthew Jackson)

The plush interior of *Huskisson*, lined out in French grey cloth with lace and trimmings to match.

James Scott Walker waxed lyrical:

> The most costly and elegant contain three apartments, and resemble the body of a coach (in the middle) and two chaises, one at each end, the whole joined together. [They are] handsome and commodious coaches, all of which are hung on springs, and run each on four equally sized wheels...

Sadly, no known contemporary depiction of the coupé-ended vehicles has been traced. The ultimate in luxury travel was by Royal Mail coach, which had a central compartment seating four, as well as a 'half compartment or coupé'. The Liverpool & Manchester had at least three mail coaches. The *Manchester Guardian* reported that the mail coaches could be converted into 'bed carriages':

> They have four seats in each compartment; and the contrivance by which one of the compartments is convertible to a bed carriage ... is a very desirable one to the invalid or valetudinarian, whom necessity obliges to travel. The backs are taken out of the seats on one side, opening into a sort of boot, lined with black leather and cushioned, and are then laid down across the space between the back and front seats, into which they fit, thus forming a complete bed. The cushions on the opposite side are buttoned up and form a pillow; the legs are put into the boot, and the passenger may thus sleep or recline comfortably.

The 'standard' first-class coach had three compartments, each seating six, as one early traveller wrote in September 1830:

> The carriages which consisted of ... three bodies, similar in interior arrangements to the French diligence, lined and fitted up in the most airy and elegant manner, and constructed with reference to the unobstructed view of passengers while on the road.

As each of the first-class (or glass) coaches was individually named, it has been possible to create a list of at least twenty-six vehicles. At least two of them, *Royal William* and *Queen Adelaide*, were curtain coaches – the end compartments were not glazed and could be closed by leather curtains. These two were ordered to be converted to glass coaches by the Board in 1832.

## Size and Weight

Early carriages were small and light. There was insufficient room to stand up in them; the passenger climbed in and sat down, rather like a modern car, or a Victorian stagecoach. They were light for two reasons: firstly, as early locomotives were not very powerful, and secondly, because the law said so. The Liverpool & Manchester Railway Act stipulated that 'no carriage [shall] be used upon the railway whose weight, inclusive of its load, should exceed four tons'.

In the David and Goliath battle between the rival Manchester & Birmingham (David) and Grand Junction Railway (Goliath), the latter used this clause – which had been 'copied from the original Acts of the Liverpool & Manchester into almost all subsequent Railway Acts' – to prevent the M&B from running over GJR to Birmingham because the M&B carriages weighed 4 tons 4 cwt. Thomas Ashton, the M&B chairman, therefore appealed to the Board of Trade. HM Inspector of Railways noted that clause was in effect 'dead letter', as most carriages weighed over four tons:

> The usual weight of passenger-carriages of the most approved construction, being upwards of four tons, exclusive of the usual load, which may be estimated at nearly two tons additional.

HM Inspector further noted that the increased weight of railway carriages, far from making them less safe, made them safer due to their sturdier construction. A clause was thus inserted

A rare survivor! A Bodmin & Wadebridge first- and second-class composite dating from the early 1830s. It measures only 14 feet long, 6 feet 6 inches wide and 8 feet 5 inches from the top of the rails to the roof.

A third-class brake coach from the Bodmin & Wadebridge Railway. It was 10 feet long, 6 feet 4 inches wide and weighed only 1 ton 19 cwt.

into the Regulation of Railway Act, 'legalising the use of carriages of a greater weight than four tons upon railways', subject to 'such regulations as should be made by the directors' and 'approved by the Board of Trade'. This passed into law in July 1842.

## Carriage Building – The Underframe

Building a railway carriage required a panoply of trades: blacksmiths, carpenters, upholsterers, leather workers, glaziers and painters. The underframes were usually made from seasoned oak or ash, although the Liverpool & Manchester did experiment with iron underframes in around 1830. Wheels were invariably mounted with outside axle boxes and journals. The Liverpool & Manchester had experimented with inside axle boxes, putting the spoked wheels outside the frame, but these were soon dismissed on the grounds of safety.

In the second generation of Liverpool & Manchester carriages, built by John Melling of Manchester from 1837, the frames consisted of:

> Two pieces of timber, kept apart ... three inches by studs, and secured by bolts. The latter mode of constructing the framing ... is for the purpose of applying ... buffer apparatus.

The replica coaches built at Derby by the LMS in 1930 for the railway centenary were drawn up from a model built by the LNWR in 1911, the working drawings of which were taken from Nathaniel Worsdell's prize-winning model of *Experience*, which he built in 1838. Sadly, Worsdell's model had been destroyed by fire while on display in Brussels in 1910. The replicas measure 15 feet 6 inches over head-stocks. The underframes are 6 feet 7 inches wide, the body is 5 feet 6 inches high and it has a maximum width of 6 feet 6 inches.

An early colour postcard of Nathaniel Worsdell's award-winning model of *Experience*, built in 1838 and sadly destroyed by fire in 1910.

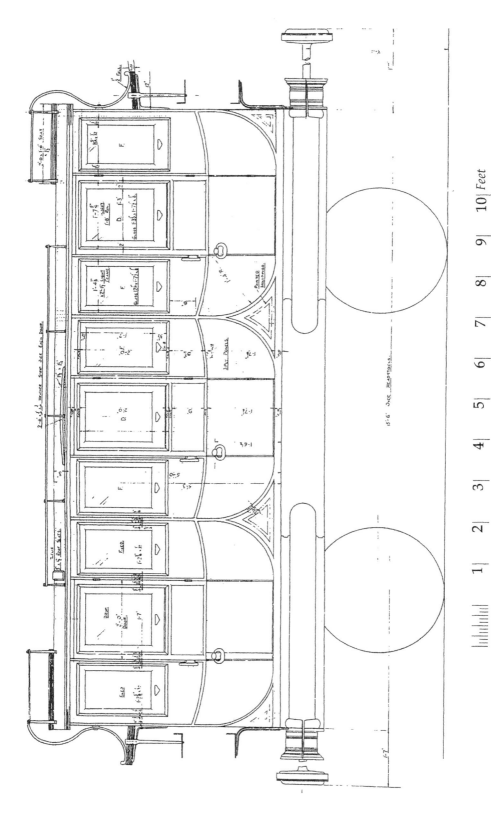

*Above and overleaf:* Drawings prepared by the LMS at Derby for the six replica Liverpool & Manchester close coaches. Scale in Feet.

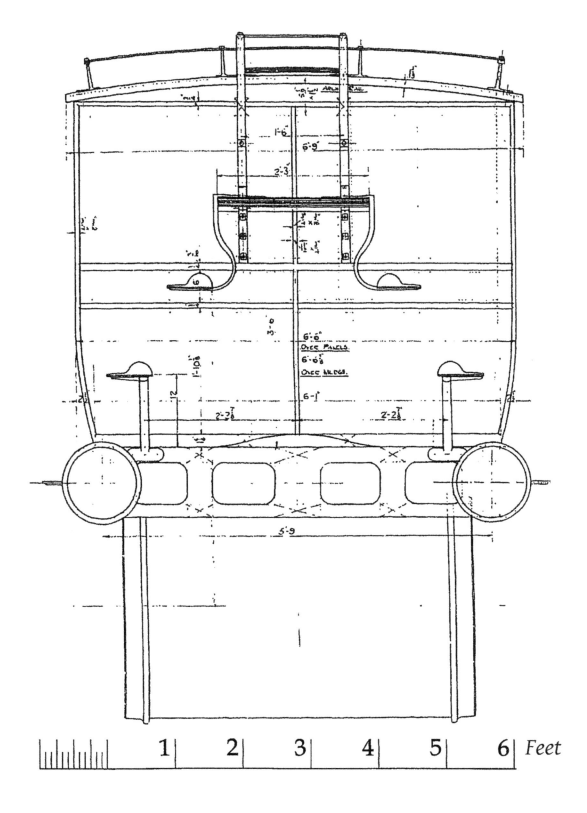

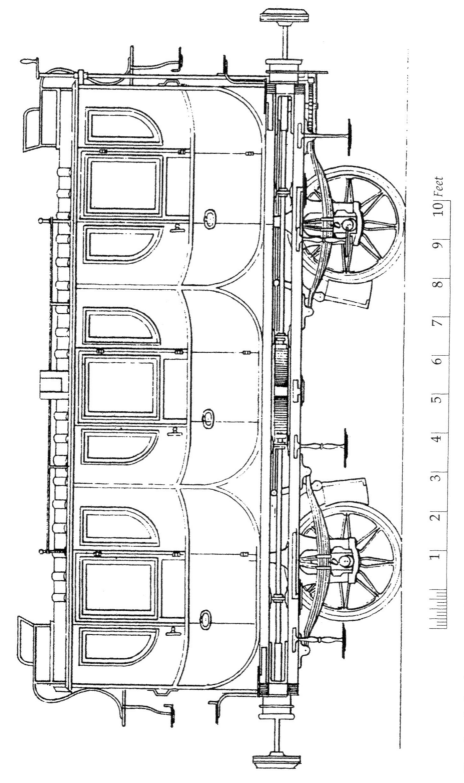

Elevation of a London & Birmingham first class coach, 1838. (Peter Chatham)

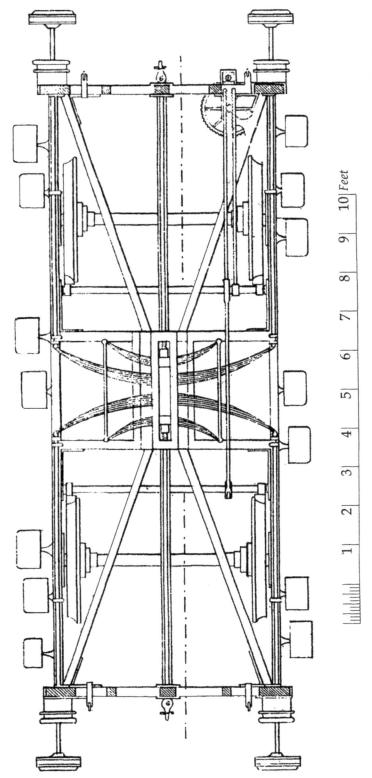

A London & Birmingham first-class carriage underframe, showing the complicated springs and rodding of Henry Booth's patent draw and buffing gear. (Peter Chatham)

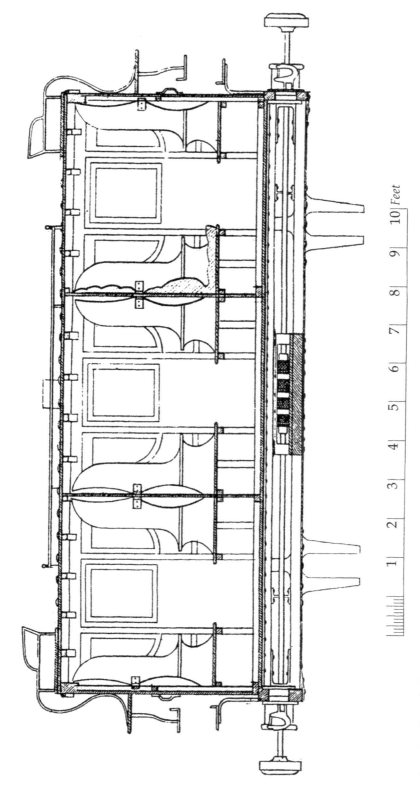

A section through the centre line of a London & Birmingham first-class coach, showing details of the compartments and seating. (Peter Chatham)

1 2 3 4 5 6 7 8 9 10 *Feet*

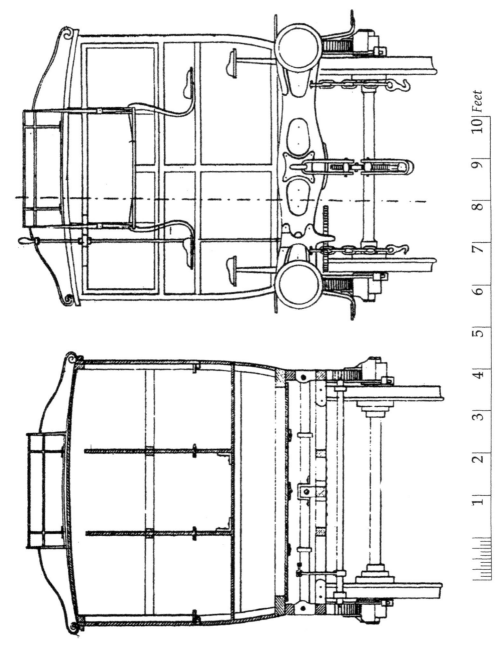

An end view and transverse section of a London & Birmingham first-class coach. (Peter Chatham)

An elevation of a London & Birmingham mail coach; note the large mail box carried on the roof. Those of the Grand Junction were identical. (Peter Chatham)

We are lucky a complete specification for a London & Birmingham first-class coach, dated 25 April 1836, still exists in the National Archives, London:

UNDER CARRIAGE FRAME

Extreme length is 15 feet 8 inches, the buffers extending 1 foot 9 inches beyond at each end. The whole must be made of well-seasoned ash ...

The carriage sides (two on each side, but they may be made in two pieces, spliced in the middle, and fitted with iron bolts and nuts,) must be 3 inches square, coupled together with wrought-iron props, and corner plates, eight of the former in each carriage ... and four of the latter.

The ends of the carriage, consist of two pieces of ash, at each end, extending from side to side (6 feet 1 inch), 3½ inches wide by 3 inches thick, and swelling to 11½ inches at the deepest part, morticed together as in the sides, only with three upright blocks, of ash instead of iron. The frame is strengthened by four diagonal and two centre longitudinal and two centre cross-stays, of ash, each 3 inches by 2½ inches, extending from the lower carriage, side morticed into a solid piece of ash, in the middle of the frame, 2 feet 3 inches by 1 foot 4 inches, secured thereto, as well as to the carriage sides, by strong angle plates of wrought iron, and plated at the corners with wrought iron ... fixed on with ½ inch bolts and nuts. The whole of the lower carriage side, must be plated throughout on one side with wrought iron, 3/8ths of an inch thick, 2¾ inches wide, and fixed in the same manner as the corner plates, with bolts and nuts. The total weight of the plating will be about two hundred weight, and twenty pound, and that of the bolts and nuts (about 350 of each) one hundred [weight], two quarters.

# Wheels and Running gear

Wheels were cast iron with wrought-iron tyres; Wishaw (1839) records them as being 3 feet in diameter on most lines. The model of the Liverpool & Manchester coach *Experience* suggests an 8-foot wheelbase – the wheels being located under the divisions between the compartments. The London & Birmingham specification states:

There must be four axle guards, of wrought iron, tapering from ¾ of an inch to 5-8ths of an inch thick, firmly fixed to the carriage sides by bolts and nuts, in exact square with each other, at the distance of 8 feet 6 inches from centre to centres ... There must be eight wrought iron roller boxes [for the leaf springs], weighing, with rollers for the same, three quarts of a hundred weight; these are to be screwed under the part of the carriage side, the extremities of the sides or bearing springs to rest and work upon.

WHEELS, AXLES, AXLE BOXES, AND SPRINGS

The wheels must be made with the rim and spokes of wrought iron, and the nave of cast iron ... The outer rim or tyre to be tapped on the inner rim with not less than eight screw-bolts and nuts in each wheel.

The axle to be made of the best rolled or wrought iron, 3 inches in diameter in the centre, 3½ inches where it passed through the nave, and to be turned down to 2 inches and 5-8ths, for an outside bearing of 4½ inches long, which must be case-hardened. The wheels to be firmly keyed to the axle, with a 5-8th of an inch key, and the tire to be turned ... To be painted and picked out with one coat of paint and a coat of varnish. The weight of the four wheels and axle boxes is about eighteen hundred weight.

The axle boxes, which are of cast iron, must be fitted up with brasses ... to suit the journals. Upon the axle boxes are fixed the side or bearing springs, of which there are four [in total], having each twelve plates, ¼ inch steel, 3 inches wide, and ... 5 feet long; the weight of the four is about three hundred weight one quarter and fourteen pounds.

# Buffing and Draw Gear

The very earliest rolling stock had solid ('dumb') buffers and un-sprung draw gear, loose-coupled with three chains. It is no wonder that enginemen were urged to start their trains slowly and gently, not only to prevent these chains from breaking, but also to take up the slack slowly in order to bring the entire train into movement and prevent the vehicles banging against each other as each one began to move. Nicholas Wood explained this problem in 1838:

> The inertia of one wagon, by any change of motion, is independent of the other; and therefore when the engine puts the first carriage in motion, it is done by a jerk, or sudden pull, and so on throughout the whole train as each carriage is successively put in motion; and, consequently, a succession of jerks is felt by the passengers ... Again, when the train is stopped, or the speed slackened, the inertia of each carriage causes it to strike against the preceding one ... and thus the passengers are continually subjected to a succession of jerks, or shocks, whenever any change of motion takes place.

To partially overcome this, early sprung buffers consisted of a buffer head (a turned disc of solid ash, around 14 inches in diameter), onto which was fixed a tail rod passing through the buffer beam. Between the wooden buffer head and buffer beam was a large coiled spring. The spring was protected by a leather sleeve, stuffed with horse hair. Sprung draw gear was adopted, again using a coiled spring, which was compressed under tension as the load was taken up.

It was the ever-resourceful Henry Booth, General Superintendent of the Liverpool & Manchester Railway, who developed sprung buffing and draw gear, as well as the three-link screw coupling. Booth mounted his buffers on long iron rods, which ran longitudinally, acting on the end of a large elliptical leaf-spring. Similarly, the draw-hook worked a tail rod, connecting with a smaller leaf spring. Booth patented this idea, together with his three-link screw coupling, in January 1836. In order to keep the vehicles closely coupled so that their buffers were always touching, Booth did away with loose coupling and instead adopted a much shorter three-link chain, the central link of which was a screw-link, which was used to shorten or lengthen the chain:

> The screw is turned until the buffer heads are brought together; when the screw is turned round two or three times more, until their ends [the buffers], pressing against the springs of the carriage, produce a pressure against each other, equal to about a fourth or fifth of the elasticity of the springs.

Naturally, this system of buffing and draw gear was adopted by the Liverpool & Manchester, and subsequently by the Grand Junction and the London & Birmingham. Henry Booth hoped that his invention:

> [Would] give steadiness and smoothness of motion, at rapid speeds, which they have not when the buffers of each carriage are separate from those of the adjoining carriage.

T. F. Bergin of the Dublin & Kingstown Railway did away with the 'complicated springs, levers, and bars' in favour of a series of coil springs, upon which the buffing and draw acted. Coil rather than leaf springs were adopted by the Newcastle & Carlisle Railway, by their chief engineer, Mr Blackmore.

One major problem was that most railways – other than those that connected with the Liverpool & Manchester – adopted their own standard buffer height and spacing, and as late as 1847, one correspondent to *The Times* noted:

> The buffers of every carriage ought to be exactly the same height from the ground. If those on one carriage are lower than those of the carriage before it, the unavoidable consequence,

if a concussion take place, must be that the lower buffers will have a tendency to throw the preceding carriages upwards ...

Every carriage ought to be provided with a break. Let the experiment be made to prove how much shorter a space a train so provided could be safely stopped, than a train as usually provided with breaks.

A mode of signalling to the driver by the guards, and between the guards and passengers. For the former, a few pre-arranged notes on the bugle would suffice; for the latter a bell of sufficient power might be placed in every carriage ... Signals might easily be arranged, by which the drivers intimate when every break should be vigorously applied.

# Brakes – An Optional Extra

The Liverpool & Manchester considered brakes to be an optional extra and only fitted brakes 'in the proportion of two out of every five' carriages. In other words, in each rake of five carriages, only the front and rearmost vehicles had brakes, which were worked by the 'under guard' (seated on the foremost carriage, facing backwards) and the 'upper guard' (on the rearmost carriage, facing forwards). Because locomotives only had relatively weak hand brakes (in effect, parking brakes), if the engineman wanted the brakes putting on he would sound the whistle with three short blasts; three long blasts signified to take them off. It was because of this limited braking ability that the Liverpool & Manchester ran short, light and relatively fast trains of five or six vehicles into the 1840s, with the Gauge Commissioners remarking on the shortness of their trains in 1845. Similarly, the Grand Junction and the London & Birmingham concluded that:

It is not necessary that every carriage should be provided with a break, this must be considered an extra ... [The brake] to act on both sides of the two wheels on the same side simultaneously.

The guard was responsible for the safety of the entire train; before starting, he was to make sure that:

The carriages are properly coupled, that the requisite number of break carriages are on, in the situations assigned for them, and in proper working condition; that the luggage is properly and safely stowed, and that the requisite number of tarpaulins are securely fastened over it, so as to insure it being kept perfectly dry. He should ascertain that his parcels and documents of every kind are placed in the situations assigned for them; that the roof and signal lamps are attached in their proper places, and in efficient order; and that the carriages are in a proper state of cleanliness, reporting every deficiency, in these respects, to the foreman of the porters ... Before he begins to pack his luggage on the train, on first preparing to start, he should send round his under guard to examine and report to him that all the grease boxes are filled ... He should carefully inspect the condition of every train, and never attempt to move it till he is perfectly satisfied of the safety of every part. He should use all the vigilance in his power to prevent rubbish or obstructions of any kind from being put on the line; and he should give constant attention, not only to the brakes, but to the wheels, grease boxes, and other parts of the machinery of the carriages which come under his notice; reporting any negligence or imperfections which he may observe ...

On the move, the guards were:

Responsible for the safety and regularity of the whole, notifying to the engine-man when he is going too quick, or too slow, and reporting whether he increases or lessens his speed in consequence, that due inquiries may be made into the reason for the irregularity; this notification he should make through his under guard, by signal, without leaving his place; for instance, his right hand extended, may indicate that the train is going too slow; and his left, that it is going too fast; and either arm held perpendicularly over his head should signify that the train is to be instantly stopped. While making this signal, he puts on the brake with the other hand. He should not repeat the signal that the train is going too slow, except after a lapse of some minutes, as the engine-man may have good reasons for proceeding at a cautious rate, which the guard may not know, and which might render it improper to urge him to a greater speed.

In applying the brakes, the guards were not to screw them down so tight as to 'scotch' the wheels, but to apply them gradually so that the train did not slip on the rail – or set the wooden brake blocks on fire!

## Bodywork

The frame for the bodywork was made from English ash (around 3 inches square) for strength and lightness, tennoned and dowelled together 'in a skeleton form'. The 1836 London & Birmingham specification makes this clear:

> Each body is to consist of three bodies, or compartments ...the extreme length *outside measure*, being 15 feet 6 inches; the length of each body 4 feet 11 inches, the breadth 6 feet, and the height from floor to roof 4 feet 6½ inches, all *inside measure*, and exclusive of stuffing.
>
> The frame-work of the bodies must be made of well-seasoned ash, of the following dimensions: for the bottom sides [horizontal timbers which formed the foundation of the body] 2½ inches by 4½ inches; standing pillars at the corners and doorways (twenty in the three bodies [i.e. ten per side]) 2½ inches, with a sweep 3 inches at the widest part, and the turn-under 2½ inches. The standing pillars in the doorways being strengthened at the bottom by uprights [elbows] of birch, firmly screwed to the seat rail; the top rails 2½ inches by 1½ inch; cross bars for the two ends (four in each) 2¼ inches by 2 inches with [upright] battens of ash between, 2½ inches by 1½ inch, and not less than twelve of them at each end. The cross bars across the divisions (one for each) 2½ inches by 1 inch, and the seat rails (ten in three bodies) 1½ inch by 2½ inches. The sides to be battened with ash of the same strength, and in the same manner, as the ends of the coach.

The body panels, usually made from Honduras mahogany:

> Are blocked to the framing with canvas and glue; they are grooved into the lower side and end rails; and the corner and door pillars: they are jump-jointed over the battens, and the joints covered with beads. The edges of the beads, and in general all projecting edges, are rounded– off to dislodge dust and water.

To stop the panels from splitting as they were pinned in place, they were backed with hessian:

> The panels, before being fixed, to be covered with canvas, glued on, and when fixed, which must be done with copper sprigs, 1 inch apart, they must have glued on them a second lining of canvas.

In order to save weight, many builders used *papier-mâché* to skin the carriage sides (the Victorian equivalent of MDF), but with mahogany ends for strength and stability. All the panel joints were covered with hard wood moulding. This served an important function: not only did it cover any joins in the panels, but because of its rounded shape, any water would run off, rather than percolating into the joint or sitting on a horizontal surface where it might pool, leading to rotting. On the Manchester & Birmingham and London & Birmingham, brass trim was used in areas around doors that would be particularly prone to wear and damage. In order to pull the bodywork together, wet canvas was stretched over the outside of the body and were glued in place using size, a glue usually made from cow bones.

## Roofs

Roofs were supported by a series of transverse ribs, usually ash. On top of this were laid pine tongue-and-groove boards, laying longitudinally and glued and screwed to the ribs. In order to create a smooth surface, the boards were sanded and filled before being given a coat of lead primer. The roof boards were wider than the body sides in order to 'cast off the water' and a lead rain-strip ran the length of the roof. The joint between the roof and bodyside was usually filled with a decorative half-round moulding.

> The hoop sticks [ribs] to support the roof (four in the two end bodies and three in the middle body) 2 ¼ inches wide by 1 inch and 5-8ths thick; the sides to be battened ash of the same strength, and in the same manner, as the end of the coach ... [the roof boards] of American Pine ... ¾ of an inch.

The London & Birmingham called for three hides 'weighing not less than thirty-eight pounds each' to cover the roof, 'protected on the top with ribs of ash screwed on, 3 inches apart, 2 ¼ inches broad and by 5-8ths of an inch thick'. The roof was 'bound with beading of ash, 1 ½ inch square.' This beading acted as rain-strip, 'somewhat higher over the doors ... so as to allow the rain to drop clear of the panels' and direct the water to the ends of the carriages via lead spouts at each corner. The leather was put on wet, and then was stretched and glued to the roof:

> A large wet hide of undyed leather, called Russet leather, is then placed upon the roof, and down the sides and ends of the body as low as the centre line: this is moulded by pressure, exactly to the form of the roof and panels intended to be covered, and when dry is painted with black Japan.

D. K. Clark, writing in the 1850s, preferred a leather-covered roof to the newer practice of canvas 'impregnated with white lead' as it was more hard-wearing, especially when luggage was carried on the roof, albeit more expensive. The use of black Japanned leather for the roof and upper side panels is why many contemporary prints of the Liverpool & Manchester Railway (and other) first-class coaches depict them with black upper panels.

On top of the roof were seats for the guard and an iron luggage rack:

> Seats, at both ends of the roof ... with iron seat rails; three [iron] steps on each side [sic, end], and two iron handles covered with leather at each end to mount; and a foot-board of birch, supported underneath with iron stays.
>
> The roof, for the space of 8 feet 6 inches, to be fenced along and across with luggage rails, 5-8ths of an inch in diameter, of iron, supported at intervals with uprights 4 ½ inches high, and an oiled canvas luggage sheet, with straps complete ... to extend over the same.

## Flooring

Floorboards were either pine or elm, 'usually 2¾ inches thickness, laid diagonally to cross each other' or 'longitudinally and transversally, and screwed together'. The two layers laid across each other provided a strong and robust floor. On the London & Birmingham, the floorboards were 'American Pine ... 1¼ inch [thick], plated underneath with three strap plates of wrought iron, 1½ inch wide by a ¼ of an inch thick from end to end, [and] secured by about one hundred clip-headed bolts and nuts'.

# Windows

Windows were made from plate glass, as opposed to window glass – the former being more expensive. Both sorts of glass originated with the blowing of a glass cylinder that was cut open to create a 'half pipe', which were then heated again and flattened out. This was termed 'window glass.' In 'plate glass', these flattened sheets were put on a Plaster of Paris plate – hence the term plate glass – and were then highly polished, giving them a smooth surface devoid of any of the ripples and most of the bubbles of ordinary window glass. Interestingly, a description of Grand Junction Railway coaches in 1837 states the use of single-pane windows as being an 'innovation', suggesting that previously the windows were made from multiple panes of glass, rather like a Georgian sash window, and as depicted by Nicholas Wood (1838).

The windows in the carriage doors were 'drop-lights'; i.e. they slid up and down within the thickness of the door, the movement being controlled by a leather strap. On the London & Birmingham, the drop-lights had to:

> Be of good plate glass, 22 ½ inches by 19 inches, and not less than 5-16ths of an inch thick; and the frames to be made of well-seasoned oak, 1 ½ inch broad, and to be covered [internally] with strong black velvet, or painted, filled up, pumiced, and varnished as may be required [outside]; small leather pads, stuffed with horse hair, to be put upon the bottom of the glass stop, for the glass to fall upon when let down.

## Finishes – External and Internal

The finish of railway carriages, especially those of the first class, was a work of art. A specification for first-class carriages for the Grand Junction Railway from 1837 stated that the bodysides were to be given three coats of white lead, four coats of filler, be 'well rubbed down' between coats, and, after being 'well pumiced', was to be given a further three coats of lead undercoat, and finished with two coats of the final body colour. Finally, four coats of varnish were then applied. The London & Birmingham specified in 1836 that the painting was:

> To consist of three coats of white lead or colour, and four coats of filling up; after being pumiced, the body is to receive three more coats of the same colour, and is then to be finished with two coats of a colour to be approved of by the Directors; the upper quarters are to be painted black in like manner, and the whole body is to be varnished with four coats of the best varnish.

The undercarriage and wheels were also to be painted:

> The [under]carriage to be painted with five coats of paint, of the colour corresponding with that of the bodies, to be neatly picked out, and finished with two coats of the best varnish.

Before the four coats of varnish were applied to the bodies, any sign-writing and embellishments were added. On the Liverpool & Manchester in 1837, the bodies were painted 'deep Chrome Yellow' and:

> Each of them [are] decorated with the coats of arms of Liverpool and Manchester on a shield within a garter. The painting is exceedingly well executed, and is the work of John Mather, a self-taught artist. We particularly noticed the Royal Arms on the Guard box as being very beautiful. The whole of the carriages were finished on the premises, under the able superintendance of Mr Pownall, who presides over the carriage department.

(*Gore's Liverpool Advertiser*, 31 August 1837)

A first-class coach
of the Manchester &
Birmingham Railway by
Brown, Marshall & Co. of
Birmingham, *c.* 1842.

Detail of the beautifully sign-written company heraldry of the Manchester & Birmingham Railway.

A reconstructed interior of the Manchester & Birmingham coach. (Lauren Jaye Gradwell)

The carriages of the Manchester & Birmingham Railway were painted Prussian blue, with the moulding lined out in gilt and crimson, and on the centre door panel the company coats of arms were painted in full colours.

Those of the Sheffield, Ashton-under-Lyne & Manchester Railway were more spectacular still, being 'richly painted' with the coats of arms of Sheffield, Ashton and Manchester 'in proper colours' on the lower panel of each door. Those of the Grand Junction were painted chocolate brown below the waist, with the traditional black Japanned upper panels. Designed by Nathaniel Worsdell, they were singled out as being some of the best – if not *the* best – carriages in use on any railway in the late 1830s:

> They are superb. Everything in the shape of elegance is to be found in those belonging to the
> first class... painted chocolate, and on the panels are emblazed the arms of the three towns

the railway is intended to unite [Liverpool, Manchester, Birmingham]. [They] carry eighteen passengers. The mail coaches have accommodation for four persons in each compartment; and a bed is provided for those who chose to bear the extra charge – a sovereign – for that addition to railway travelling.

(*Blackburn Standard*, 12 July 1837)

The *Manchester Courier*, which had long been a critic of the accommodation provided by the Liverpool & Manchester, thought that:

The vehicles are all beautifully finished, and are constructed in a far superior style to those on the Liverpool & Manchester road. Nothing appears to have been neglected conducive to the comfort of the passengers ... The compartment in the Mail Carriage is convertible into a bed-carriage at the pleasure of the passengers by the lifting up of one of the false backs of the carriages which forms a kind of couch.

(*Manchester Courier*, 8 July 1837)

In order to be ready for the opening in July 1837, the Grand Junction had outsourced production of its carriages: tenders were invited for carriage bodies in September 1836 for 'close coaches' (i.e. first-class) and second class, in rakes of five each, which had to conform to the drawings and patterns provided by the company. The undercarriage, wheels and brake-gear were supplied by the company, the 'breakworks to be affixed in the proportion of two out of every five.' While carriages wheels and springs appear to have been produced in-house, Joseph Locke, chief engineer of the Grand Junction, was inviting tenders in September 1836 for 400 'cast-iron wheels with malleable iron flanches, and axles keyed-on and fitted up complete', together with 800 'waggon springs.'

The North Union Railway, running between Preston and Wigan to Parkside Junction on the Liverpool & Manchester, and engineered by Charles Vignoles, opened in 1839. It painted its first-class coaches deep chrome green, with black upper panels and elaborate gilt lining-out. They were built by various carriage manufactories in the North West, with three being built across the Irish Sea in Dublin. Many of these early coaches were elegantly painted, often with elaborate heraldry of the towns the railway served (or at least hoped to):

The carriages are 30 in number, viz. 15 of the first, and 15 of the second class. Four of the first class were built and finished by Messrs. Dunn & Wise of Lancaster, and are splendidly finished with the London arms on one end, the Birmingham on the other, and those of Preston and Wigan in the centre. The accommodation in the inside, is on an improved plan, having head pieces or divisions carried upwards to the roof, and affording every comfort for the journey. Four other first class have been made by Messrs. Leece & Co of [Preston]; the plan of buffing is in the style of the Liverpool & Manchester carriages [i.e. Booth's gear]; heraldry comprises the Preston and Wigan arms on the centre door, and those of Liverpool and Manchester at each end, painted in masterly style. The elbows, or seat divisions, are made of mahogany. For beauty and strength these last four carriages are surpassed by none on any railway in the kingdom, and reflect great credit on the constructor. Four also of the first class, were made by Messrs. Jonathan Dunn of Lancaster; and the remaining three by Mr Dawson of Dublin.

(*Preston Chronicle*, 3 November 1838)

Internal appearance and fittings were as, if not more important than the lavish exterior, with railway companies hoping to attract custom away from the stagecoaches. The first-generation first-class coaches of the Liverpool & Manchester were finished in drab-coloured (light brown) wool broadcloth and:

The backs are padded and covered with fine cloth, like a private carriage ... the seats which accommodate three persons... Between the sittings is a rest for the arms, and each passenger has a cushion to himself; there is a little projection against which he may rest his head ... A passenger may sit or sleep with as much comfort as if he were in an easy chair.

(Liverpool Mercury, 11 June 1830)

The second generation of Liverpool & Manchester first-class coaches were even more splendid. In lieu of drab cloth, they were lined with French grey, 'the upholstery [being] carried to a considerable height above the seats, [with] padded head rests being included'. The trimmings were also 'French grey cloth, with buttons and lace to match'. From the description of these vehicles, it appears the first generation of coaches had no cloth lining on the inside of the doors or around the windows, while those of the second generation did:

Among the contrivances which tend to augment the comfort of the passengers, we would particularly mention the additional elbows at the sides (arm-rests on the carriage sides) and in the lining of the lights and doors in French grey cloth.

(Gore's Liverpool Advertiser, 31 August 1837)

The London & Birmingham specified that its first-class coaches be fitted up in a luxurious manner:

To be lined throughout with Drab Cloth, of a quality worth at the present time 12s 6d per yard, of 60 inches width. The quantity required for the three bodies [i.e. compartments] being about 38 yards. Lace (seven dozen [yards] for the three bodies) 18s per dozen; seaming ditto (twelve dozen) 3s 6d per dozen; pasting ditto (four dozen) 3s 6d per dozen; ... the floor to be covered with the best Brussels carpet.

The backs and cushions to be stuffed with the best curled [horse] hair, the quantity required for the three bodies being about one hundred and twelve pounds. The seats to be divided into four arms in each body, fixed on with iron corner plates and screws, and finished with broad mahogany tops, varnished; each seat also to be numbered with a Japan label, with gilt figures.

## Second Class

The Liverpool & Manchester railway equated outside passengers with second-class travel, and as a result other railway companies followed suit. The Liverpool & Manchester produced a fleet of, initially, varied roofless accommodation for its stopping trains. One contemporary description read as follows:

Those [carriages] of the second class carry twenty-four passengers, four abreast, and have seats likewise separated and numbered. The third class are open carriages, containing seats for twenty-four passengers.

While one correspondent to a Chester newspaper thought:

For the accommodation [of luggage and 'outside' passengers], there is a different kind of carriage, about as high as a common cart, and having four or six rows of seats, under which there are receptacles for the luggage; the passengers on these conveyances not being nearly so elevated, nor so much exposed to the dangers of falling off, as the outside passengers on a stagecoach.

(Chester Chronicle, 11 June 1830)

Ackerman's depiction of a modified Liverpool & Manchester second-class coach, fitted with a roof supported on iron pillars.

An alternative form of a second-class coach, with folding iron seats as well as a canopy to keep the rain off.

A traveller writing to a friend in Sheffield in October 1830 described his experience travelling second class from Liverpool to Manchester:

> I was one of the first which arrived; had my luggage put into one of the boots which are contrived under the seats, and took my place in the hindermost carriage [compartment?] with my face to the horses – I should say *to the engine* ... It may be as well to mention that some of the seats have cushions and some have not. Being myself fond of ease in travelling, I immediately noted this important distinction, and took advantage of it.

> (*Sheffield Independent*, 2 October 1830)

These open second-class carriages were described as resembling nothing more than a set of church pews on wheels:

> Panelled at each end, and the rail which supports the back so contrived that it may be turned over, so that the passengers may face either way and the machine does not require to be turned.

No specification or drawing for these early Liverpool & Manchester second-class coaches has yet come to light. Those built at Derby by the LMS in 1930 are probably based on the well-known print by Ackerman, but as the L&M second-class coaches (and its later thirds) had seats, the roofless, standing-only replicas owe more to 1930s ideas of 1830s travel than to the 1830s! They are therefore best treated with caution.

Lecount records a complete specification for a fully enclosed London & Birmingham second-class carriage. It is likely, however, that this design was either simply a proposal or was replaced early on, as the L&B provided two types of second-class accommodation: semi-opens for day use, and enclosed for night travelling.

> The second-class, should be fitted, as to wheels, axles, buffers, and iron-work, exactly the same as the first-class. The length of the coach is a little decreased [13 feet 6 inches]; it has no linings, but should have air-cushion; the three bodies [sic., compartments] are open to each other at the top and inside the carriage, it receives fewer coats of paint and varnish.

There was a hand brake and seats for four persons on the roof (including the guard). Luggage was carried both in boots under the seats and on the roof. Externally, they were to be painted:

> With 3 coats of lead colour and then filled up; 4 coats of brown ochre and white lead, and afterwards 2 coats of lead colour and 2 of the finishing colour, to be lettered in plain letters in paint, and 2 coats of good varnish, and the inside to be painted drab.

Where only two classes of carriage were in use (first and second), Lecount recommended an upgraded form of second class, using semi-open vehicles, like those of the Liverpool & Manchester:

> The second-class should have ends built up ... and a roof put on, which may be supported at each division of the body, the sides being open, or ... made to close at night, or in bad weather, at a slight increase in the fare.

Unlike the draughty semi-opens of the Liverpool & Manchester – described by the contemporary press as little better than pig pens – the enclosed second-class coaches of the Grand Junction (1837) had the same level of finish as their firsts:

> Panelled with good Bay wood, handsomely painted and varnished (four coats); the window of the door is one large pane of plate glass, and there is a smaller one, also of plate glass, (a quarter

A replica Liverpool & Manchester standing-only third-class coach, which was built at Derby by the LMS in 1930. It was probably inspired by the Ackerman plates, rather than any known contemporary drawings or models. (Matthew Jackson)

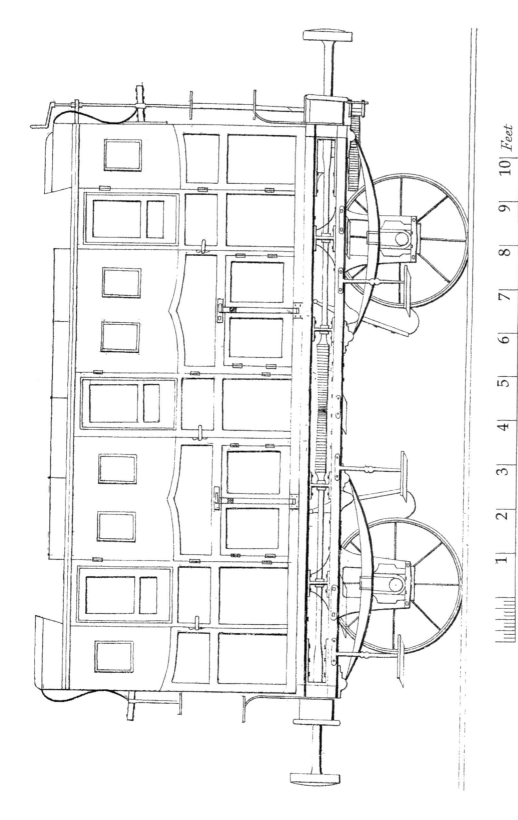

A London & Birmingham enclosed second class carriage from 1837. (Andrew Mason)

Feet

1  2  3  4  5  6  7  8  9  10

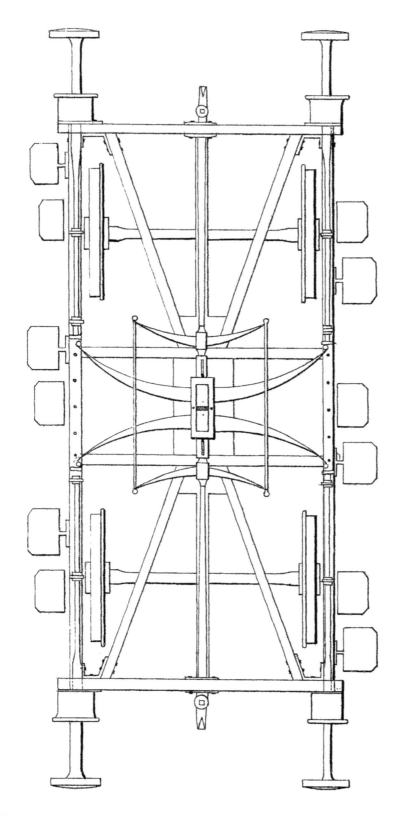

Detail of the underframe. (Andrew Mason)

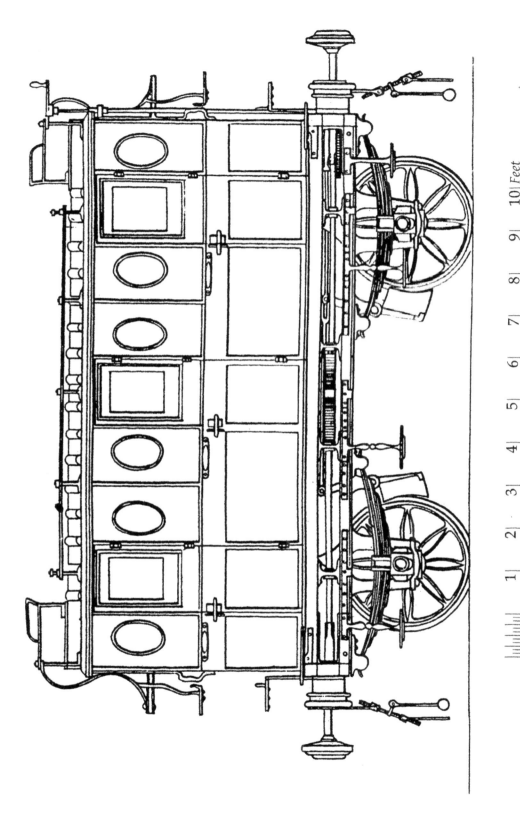

A London & Birmingham enclosed 'night second', 1837. (Peter Chatham)

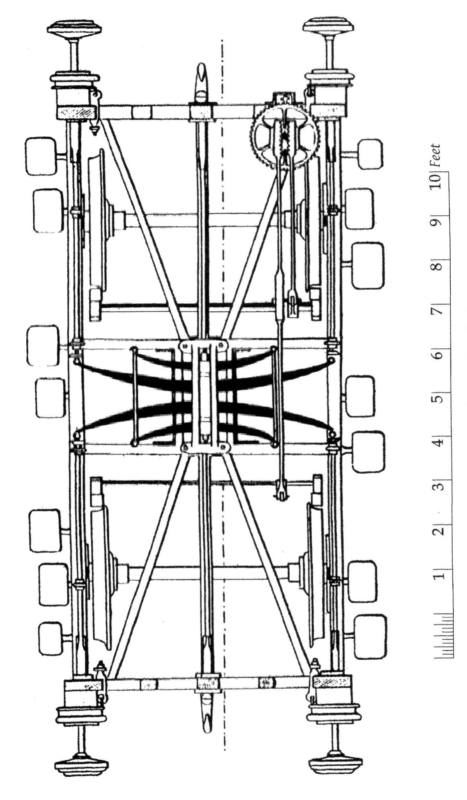

The underframe of a night second, showing the details of the buffing and brake-gear. (Peter Chatham)

1 2 3 4 5 6 7 8 9 10 *Feet*

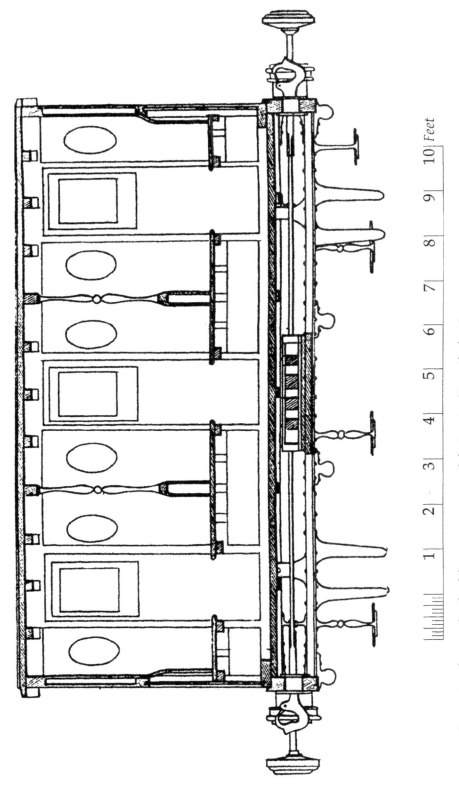

A centre-line section showing details of the compartments and the interior. (Peter Chatham)

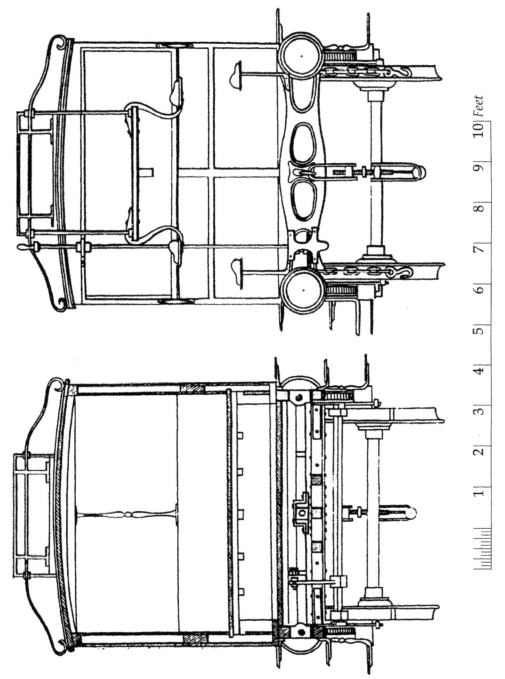

An end view (showing steps and guard's seat) and transverse section. (Peter Chatham)

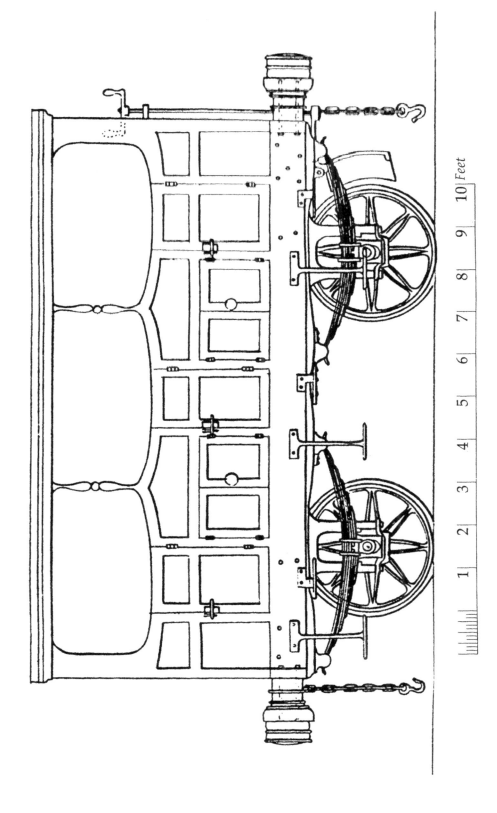

London & Birmingham semi-open 'day second', similar to those run on the Liverpool & Manchester 1830–1844. (Peter Chatham)

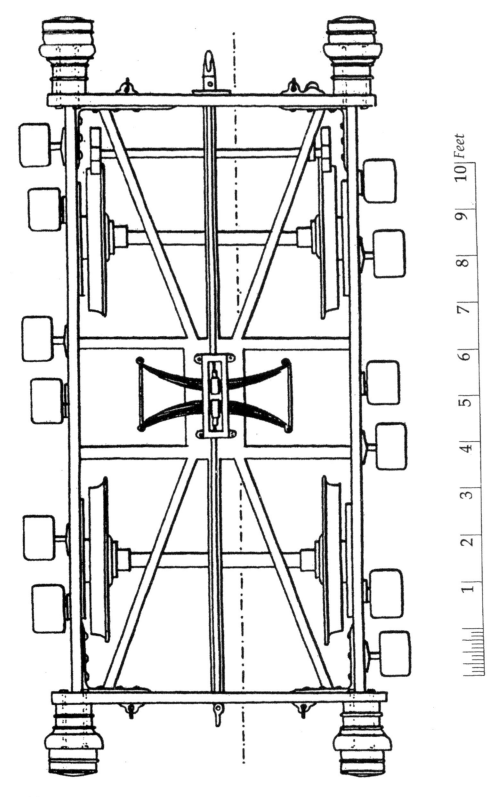

Underframe of the day second: note that only the draw-hooks are sprung. (Peter Chatham)

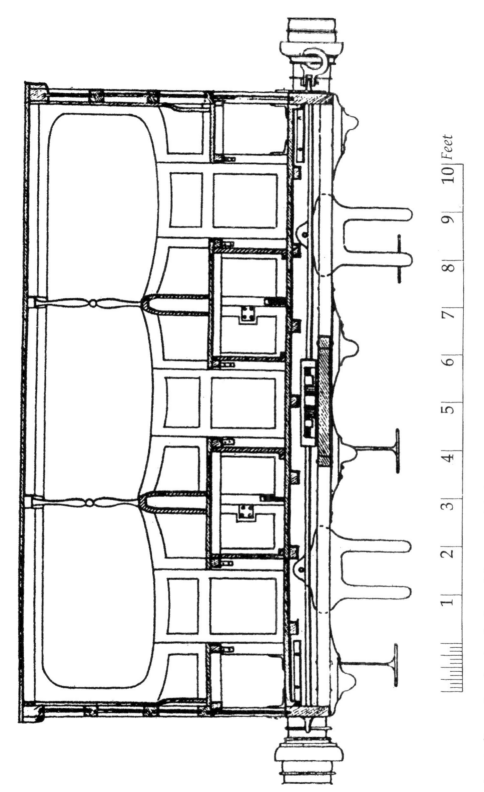

A centre-line section showing the form of the seats and the luggage boots under the seats. (Peter Chatham)

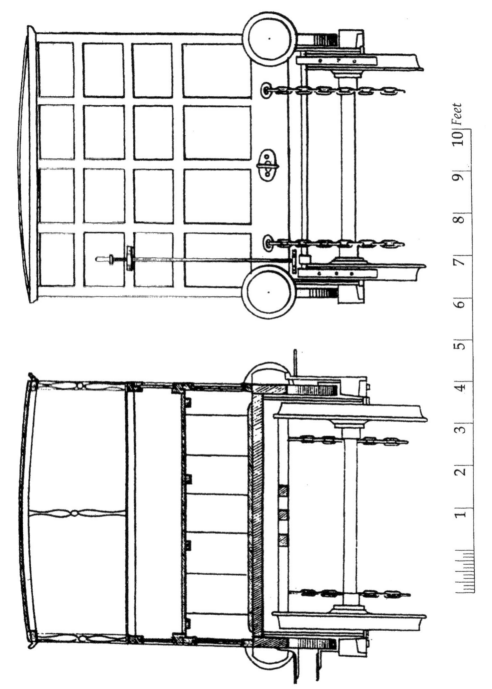

A transverse section and end view; note the brake handle and the ends 'boarded up close'. (Peter Chatham)

of an inch thick) on each side of the door, so that the passengers will sit in comfort, free from any draught, protected from the weather, without being excluded from a view of the country.

The second-class coaches of the Manchester & Birmingham (1840) had four compartments, seating twenty-eight passengers in total. They were fully enclosed but were 'open through', lacking internal partitions. Each compartment was lettered A–D and the seats were 'not cushioned or divided'. Despite being able to carry more passengers, these second-class carriages were obviously of lighter construction than first class, weighing only 3 tons 16 cwt compared to 4 tons 4 cwt. They were probably built by Brown, Marshalls & Co. of Birmingham, a company that was founded in 1840 to build railway vehicles, having originally been coachbuilders in London.

Both the Grand Junction and the Manchester & Leeds ran composite first- and second-class coaches, consisting of a central enclosed first-class compartment, flanked by two open seconds at either end.

## Third Class, Wagon Class and Parliamentary Trains

The notion of 'third class' is a pure railway invention, as it did not figure in the earlier coaching tradition, but several companies operating in densely populated, often industrial areas found that they could offer cheap accommodation at either end of the working day for those operatives who wished to travel for work. One such line, the Manchester, Bolton & Bury – which, despite its name, did not run to the latter town – was an early example of a commuter line. Opening in 1838 it offered 'wagon class' in open cars, tickets costing 1s with three trains per day, at 8 a.m., 12 noon and 7.45 p.m., the latter being a special 'workmen's train' running non-stop between the two termini. It operated the bulk of its trains around the peak rush hour periods from 7.30 a.m. to 12 noon and in the evening at 5 p.m., 6 p.m. and 7.45 p.m.

The Liverpool & Manchester considered the possibility of carrying a third class as early as 1839, largely due to pressure from neighbouring railways, such as the Manchester, Bolton & Bury and the Manchester & Leeds. W. W. Currie informed the Board in October 1839 that the Manchester & Leeds were carrying third-class passengers in open wagons, which lacked both seats and roofs. The directors, however, were afraid that if they introduced third class, with its correspondingly lower fares, then it would draw passengers away from first- and second-class trains. Introduction of third class was again discussed by the Board on 15 January 1844: initially they refused to sanction third class, pointing out that their second-class fares were lower than the new Parliamentary rate for third class. In April, however, this decision was reversed: new, enclosed second-class coaches were ordered, as this was cheaper than converting the older 'blue boxes'. These older carriages, many of which probably dated from 1830, were down-graded to third, and the first third-class train ran in October 1844, from Manchester at 6.30 a.m. and from Liverpool at 6.30 p.m.

The Manchester & Leeds, running as it did through heavily populated mill towns, ran third class from opening day and found it to be its most lucrative market. Chairman Henry Houldsworth stated as such at a special meeting of the Manchester & Leeds in October 1839:

Taking a first-class carriage and a third-class carriage, assuming that they were each two-thirds full, he found that the latter yielded a high profit, per ton, per mile, than the first-class: the one paying 7¾d. and the other 8¼d. ... independent of the outlay for the carriages, one of which cost above £400 and the other only £150, so that when a first-class wore out, it cost as much to replace it as would purchase three of the others.

(*Manchester Courier* 12 October 1839)

In other words, it was in the directors' and shareholders' interests to keep third class cheap and therefore profitable.

The Manchester & Leeds third-class stock was simple and brutal, 'having neither roof nor closed sides'. A model third-class carriage, supplied by Melling & Co. of Manchester for the

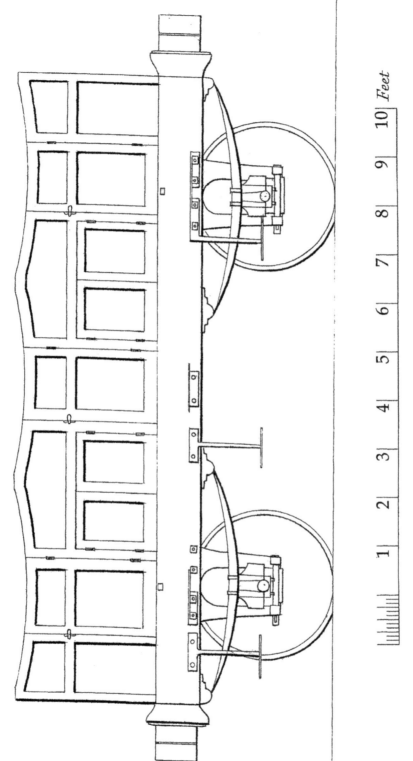

A London & Birmingham open third-class carriage from Lecount. (Andrew Mason)

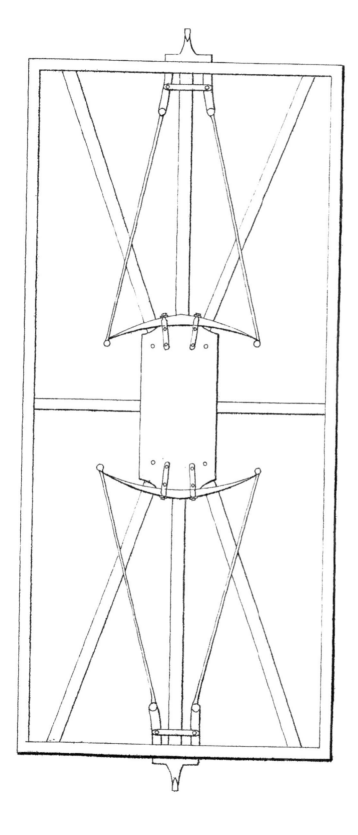

Underframe details of London & Birmingham third-class: note sprung draw-hook but dumb buffers. (Andrew Mason)

|  | 1 | 2 | 3 | 4 | 5 | 6 | 7 | 8 | 9 | 10 | *Feet* |

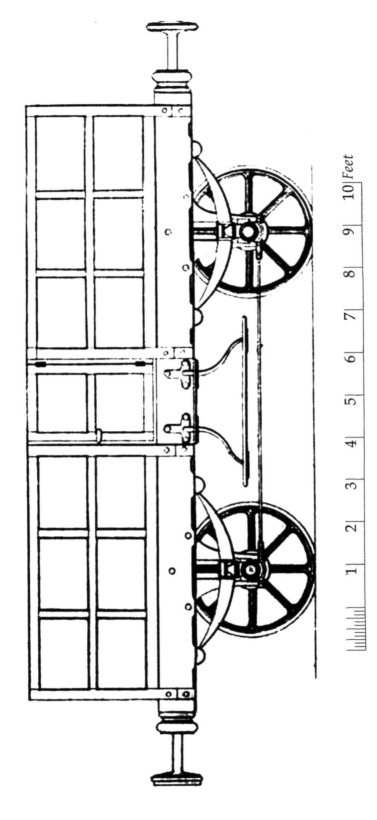

Above and opposite: A typical third-class coach, with passengers sitting on longitudinal benches but with only a single, central door on each side. (Andrew Mason).

1 2 3 4 5 6 7 8 9 10 Feet

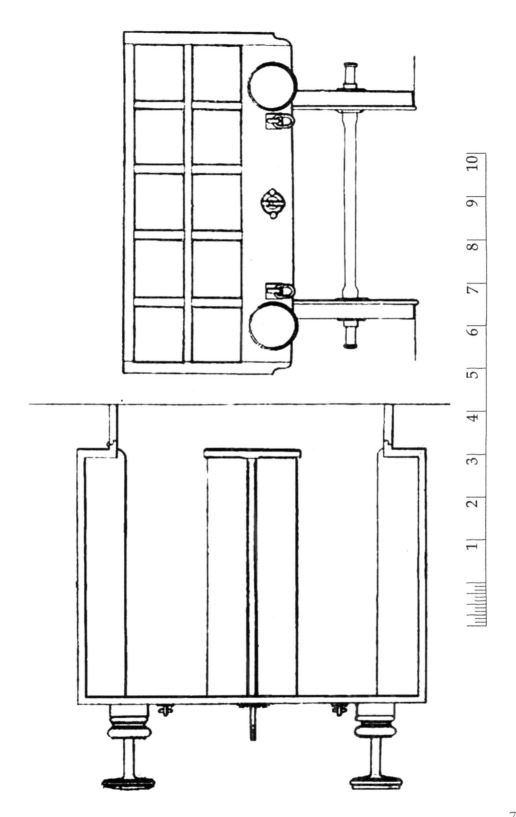

perusal of the Manchester & Leeds directors, consisted of a single long bench, upon which passengers sat, back-to-back, 'and [was] thereby rendered capable of containing 40 persons'. The *Manchester Guardian* (20 March 1839) inspected another type of Manchester & Leeds third-class carriage:

It is 17 feet 10 ½ inches in length and 7 feet 11 ½ inches in width. The form of the carriage ... more nearly resembling the form of a long boat, with the stem and stern cut off and made square. A bench seat extends the whole length of the carriage on each side, and down the middle is another broad bench, 27 ½ inches in width dividing in the middle by an open rail or back of wood rising to a height of 14 inches from the seat, so as to form two benches on which passengers sit back to back. Allowing 14 inches to each passenger, the carriage would seat about 60 persons. Ascent is had by two broad iron footplates at each corner of the carriage, so that there are four doors affording ready ingress and egress. An iron rail extends along the sides of the carriage so as to prevent ... falling over. The exterior ... is painted olive green and is formed into panels. The whole is a neat appearance, and is capable of carrying a great number of passengers than any other carriage we have seen of equal dimensions.

A full specification for a Manchester & Leeds third-class carriage, dated 1843, also exists:

The whole of the body and carriage is to be made of well-seasoned ash, except the carriage sides, which may be made of well-seasoned foreign oak, if more convenient than ash. The body is made separate from the carriage, or underframe, and is bolted thereon. The length of the carriage, including the buffer, is 19ft. 6in., the width 6ft. 2 in., all outside measure. The length of the body is 14 ft. 6 in., the width 7 ft., height 3ft., with a railing of iron 6 in. high round the body ... all outside measure.

Four doors, one at every corner of the body ... The doors to be provided with strong brass hinges, double joints, and with outside brass door handles, with spring catch, &c., and safety hooks, &c., as per pattern carriage. The whole of the pannels to be of pine, very dry, 1 in. thick, free from knots and shakes, to be well seasoned before put in, and properly canvassed when in.

The underframes were also timber, being made from solid oak:

The sides of the underframe to be made of one piece running the whole length, 10in. deep by 3 in. thick; the end bars of the same dimensions; the cross bars, in the centre, 3in. square; the upper bars, on which two of the body bars rest, is framed an inch below the top of the carriage side, to receive the bottom of the these bars are 2 ½ in. wide by 2in. thick; Diagonal bars, and also the centre bars, are 3in.thick; the diagonals are to be placed 6 in. from the carriage sides in the corner, to allow the wheels to work. The block in the centre of carriage, 13 in. wide by 3 inches thick.

The bodies and underframes were to be made in a 'workmanlike manner', and:

The whole of the wood work, as well as the iron work, to be properly put together with good white lead, and properly secured. The painting to consist of two coats of lead colour and two coats of dark olive green, to be properly picked out in black, and to receive two coats of good varnish. The inside to be painted with two coats of dark drab and varnished.

The wheels, axles and axle-boxes, while furnished by the company, were to be 'put under and properly painted' by the contractor. No brakes are mentioned in the specification. Lecount of the London & Birmingham recommended:

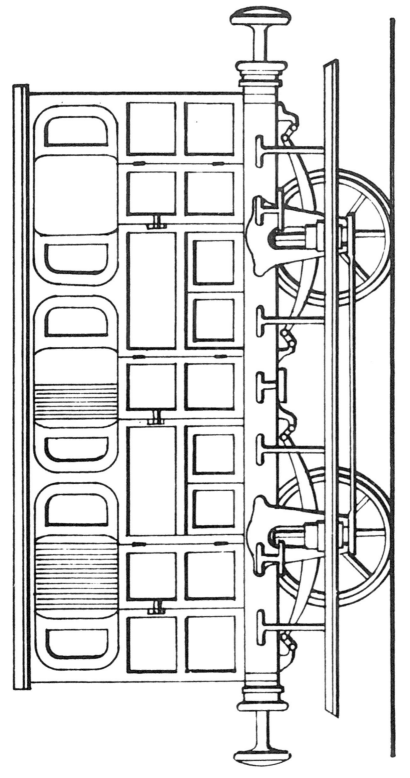

Luxury indeed! A fully enclosed third-class coach as running on the Sheffield, Ashton-under-Lyne & Manchester Railway as a result of the Gladstone Act.

The third class should be entirely open, the wheels, axles, and springs, conforming to the best, as conducing good order of the road; but there should be no buffer apparatus, only a draw-bar and spring ... Buffer blocks are to be fixed to the ends of the carriage, having an end covering of leather stuffed with horse hair.

The Sheffield, Ashton-under-Lyne & Manchester introduced new coaching stock in 1845 as a result of the Gladstone Act a year earlier. They abolished the open standing-only third-class and provided fully enclosed vehicles. The *Sheffield Iris* thought them:

Some of the most splendid carriages that ever adorned a line of Railway. To say nothing of the First and Second Class carriages, those of the Third Class are unparalleled for comfort and protection, being covered at the top and sides, and richly painted on the exterior. The guard box behind is sheltered on three sides and the top so that even in the coldest season, this important functionary will be protected from the inclemency of the weather.

# CHAPTER 3

# The Travelling Experience

Travelling in a 1830s train would have been completely different to that of today; the author, having travelled in an original Manchester & Birmingham carriage from 1840, can attest to a feeling of claustrophobia, especially at night. While a railway carriage was roomier than a contemporary stagecoach, to the modern traveller they are cramped, with little leg or head room. Once you were locked in to your compartment, that is where you remained for the entirety of your journey. Unlike on a stagecoach, where it was possible to communicate with the guard to stop the coach for a few minutes in order for a passenger to relieve themselves, this was not possible by train: a passenger in 1838 had to make sure they had been to the lavatory at home before even setting out, as there were no conveniences at the station and definitely not in the carriages.

The ride quality of these carriages can be best described as 'choppy' – with a short 8-foot wheelbase, the replica second-class coaches at MOSI or the 1930 replica vehicles at York find every joint and defect in the permanent way. Even with modern 60-foot rail laid on timber sleepers, the ride is not exactly a smooth one. In 1838, when rail lengths were 15 or 30 feet

CONVERSATIONS EN WAGON.

'Une Conversation en wagon' – a contemporary French print depicting first-class travel in the 1840s. Placing a hat or book on a seat was a well-established trick of gaining extra seclusion.

Une Conversation en wagon. — Dessin de Bertall.

and often laid on stone blocks, the effect would have been one of constant jolting and a regular 'thunk' as the wheels found the joints between the rails. This effect would have been partially lessened in an enclosed first-class carriage, but it was not so for those in the semi-open or open second- and third-class vehicles. The best modern impression of travel in a four-wheeled third-class carriage would be to ride in a Class 142 'Pacer' Railbus, at rush hour (standing room only), at speed.

Edward Mogg in his *Handbook for Railway Travellers (1838)* urged first time travellers:

> Not to leave to the last moment application for a ticket, when from the confusion consequent on a numerous assemblage, and anxious endeavour to keep the time, any mistake made in the receipt of change it may be then too late to rectify.

Mogg also urged passengers to keep their luggage to a minimum:

> The traveller whose equipage cannot be contained in a carpet bag, which may be placed under the seat he occupies, will find himself upon quitting his carriage in an enviable position, compared with whom who has to select his from that of perhaps 150 persons.

Heavy luggage – trunks etc. – went on the roof, where it was protected from the elements by heavy canvas sheets, which were held in place with wire-reinforced leather straps. Each passenger who had their luggage stowed on the roof was given a numbered ticket, which corresponded with a numbered label fixed to their luggage so that it could easily be found at the end of the journey. While luggage was manhandled onto the roofs by the porters, it was usually slid down wooden chutes (rather like as at a modern airport) to the platform below. This was one reason why many 'Handy Books' for novice railway travellers urged their readers to make sure their luggage was well packed and insured.

Robert Surtees asserted:

> Let someone keep a sharp look-out on your luggage while you take your place ... see your luggage put on the roof of the carriage you occupy, and book the number of the carriage... Carry your own provisions, by which you can dine when you are hungry, instead of when the Railway Directors think you ought to be. Chickens cut up, and tongue sliced, with bread, biscuits, cakes and so on, are most convenient.

'Your luggage, ma'am?' A cartoon by *Punch* showing the apparent chaos of the Victorian railway station. Note the guard with his elaborate cartouche pouch and the porter ringing the bell to hurry passengers up.

Passengers travelling by open (third) or semi-open (second class) carriages were urged to sit with their backs to the engine:

> By which means they will avoid the ashes therefrom, that in travelling generally, but particularly through the tunnels, prove a great annoyance; the carriage farthest from the engine will be found most desirable. Effectually, however, to guard against so great an evil, it may be found advisable perhaps to follow the practice recently introduced by the frequenters of Epsom, who in dusty weather have latterly adopted the use of the veil, the best possible protection to the face and eyes.

Compartments were devoid of heating, so passengers travelling in the dark or in winter were urged to wrap up warm:

> Railway Rugs are much in vogue for travelling, but a shepherd's plaid or maud is a much better thing, being applicable to any part of the season that is cold, and convertible into a counterpane at night. Caps and wraps of all sorts are to be had at the principle stations; but the less healthy people coddle and wrap themselves the better.

One letter-writer to the *Morning Post* (6 October 1840) offered hints to the would-be railway traveller on the London & Birmingham route:

1. Never travel by night
2. Occupy the centre seat in the centre compartment of the central carriage of the train; the motion is less; you cannot by accident thrust your head or arms out of the window; the majority of travellers chose the seat by the window. Consequentially there is an even chance you can rest your legs on the seat opposite. If the carriage is upset in the case of accident, always sit opposite a large matron, but ensure she has removed her stays as the chance of serious injury is much reduced.
3. Always compel the porters to place your luggage on the roof of the carriage that contains *you*; any small parcel under your seat …
4. Never go by the first morning train.
5. Always select the fast train – the word 'fast' only signify better conducted, and that you will stop four, instead of fourteen times between London and Birmingham.
6. Avoid the society of old nurses, and their accompaniments like you would the plague. If you cannot change your carriage, go by another train.
7. Be very careful what you eat. At Wolverton best avoid the Pork Pies especially; very few pigs are brought up in the neighbourhood.
8. Always arrive at the station half an hour before the time. You can then choose your seat, and guard against being locked up in the wrong carriage…
9. Never pay the servants of the establishment; but do not fail to compliment them or complain or any incivility or insult.
10. Never smoke: never sleep.
11. If you have shares in the railways: sell them.

The following 'Hints for All Rail Travellers' appeared in *The Railway Times:*

> Pack up your luggage in such order that you can readily carry with you the small matters that you may want on your journey, or immediately on your arrival; let the rest be put in such trunks, cases, boxes, or other packages as will effectually protect it … remembering that at railway station a good deal of business must be done in a little time, and, therefore, luggage … gets rough usage.
>
> Let your name and destination appear legibly on your luggage … put your name and address inside also of each package …

Daumier's take on the evils of smoking in railway carriages.

Be at the station some minutes before the time; if you do not resolve to be so, expect the train to be on its way without.

Get your ticket by paying your fare, and be careful to understand exactly how far that ticket frees you. On some railways you keep the ticket to the end of your journey; on others you are called for it on your starting. In either case be ready with it, remember that if you cannot produce it, you may be called upon to pay your fare again.

Expect to pay for the carriage of all your luggage above 56lbs. weight.

Take the best care that you can to prevent the necessity of you leaving the compartment before you reach the refreshment station at the end of your journey.

Take your seat as soon as you have made all your needful arrangements; if you have other luggage with you, let it not be so bulky as to annoy your fellow passengers.

Do not open the carriage door yourself; and do not, at any station, except those where refreshments are provided, attempt to leave the carriage for any reason whatever and without the knowledge of the conductor, lest you be injured by some accident, or left behind.

Neither smoking nor dogs are allowed in the carriages; the latter are carried under proper arrangements, and at a small charge ...

Female attendants will be found at each terminus, and at the refreshment station, to wait upon the ladies and the children.

Before a passenger could board their carriage, the carriages to be prepared and cleaned, both internally and externally. Francis Head described the process on the LNWR in the 1840s:

Two greasy-faced men in canvas jackets, with an oil-can ... and with something like a mophead of dirty cotton ... diligently wipe ... the dust and perspiration from the buffer-rods of the ... carriage[s]. As soon as these irons are perfectly clean and dry rubbed, they oil them from their can ... Two others in green jackets – on one each side of the carriage – who deal solely in a yellow composition of tallow and palm-oil. Carrying a wooden box full of this ointment in one hand, and a sort of short flat salve-knife in the other, the open with the latter the small iron trap-doors which cover the receptacles for greasing the axles, restore whatever quantity has been exhausted.

While the mechanical parts of the carriages were being attended to, the bodywork was cleaned and prepared:

> The Carriage 'Searcher' ... enters every carriage, lifts up first all the stuffed blue seats, next the carpet, and then, inquisitively peeping under the two seats, he leaves the carriage laden with whatever article or articles may have been left in it ... On the roof ... there sits aloft a man called a 'Strapper' whose sole duty it is, on the arrival of every train, to inspect, clean, shampoo and refresh with cold-drawn neat's-foot oil the luggage straps ... It is the especial duty of this inquisitor to condemn any straps that may be faulty, in order that they may be immediately replaced.

As soon as this was done, the carriages were to be uncoupled and shunted by hand onto the carriage roads between the departure and arrival platforms. It was here that the carriages were washed with soap and water, and then polished to a shine by a gang known as 'moppers':

> A 'first-class mopper' would on no account demean himself by mopping a second-class carriage, and in like manner a 'second-class mopper' only attains that distinction after he has for a sufficient length of time been commissioned to mop horse-boxes and common luggage-trains.

After the carriages had been washed and polished, 'a small army of he-housemaids', with a cloth, a chamois leather, a brush and a dust-pan, cleaned the windows, 'wipe[d] the woodwork, brushe[d] the blue cloth seats, sides, and backs'. The carriages were then inspected and, with the carriages 'reported fit to depart', they were 'marshalled into trains', where they stood ready to accept their next load of passengers.

## Breaking the Sabbath

Sunday travelling by railway caused considerable controversy, which was led principally by Sir Andrew Agnew MP (Wigtownshire), who pressed not only for a ban on Sunday travelling, but all secular labour on Sundays. Supported by Scottish Presbyterians, he tried unsuccessfully to introduce four Bills into Parliament, which would have forced people to attend a religious service and barred them from doing any work. For some reason, it was the railways, and the locomotive in particular, that drew religious scorn. In Manchester, one Roman Catholic clergyman claimed that railways ran contrary to the will of God because they were 'unnatural', and therefore sinful, while the stagecoach, horse or river boat was not. Another minister thought the railway locomotive itself was sinful, being the 'work of human hands alone', while one Evangelical in Sheffield believed that the railway locomotive was predicted in the Bible as the 'pillar of fire' of Exodus, which led the Israelites during their wilderness years. The largely Quaker proprietors of the Birmingham & Gloucester Railway refused to sanction any train on Sundays other than the legally mandated mail train.

Opposition to Sabbatarianism came notably from the Unitarians. Rev. William Gaskell, Minister of Cross Street Unitarian Chapel, led the anti-Sabbatarian crusade in Manchester, arguing that to prevent persons from travelling on Sundays, especially the working classes, was un-Christian. Enabling people to leave the dirty, cramped city for the hills was not only good for them physically, but mentally, emotionally and spiritually. Gaskell argued in favour of opening public parks, galleries and museums on Sundays for the same reason: Sunday was indeed a day of rest, but also of recreation, to feed the mind and soul.

After the Bishop of Hereford proposed a clause to prohibit Sunday travel on the Newcastle & Carlisle Railway, 347 dissenters (i.e. Unitarians) sent a petition to Parliament 'praying the House not to insert any clause in the Newcastle and Carlisle Railway Bill prohibiting travel on the Sabbath'. Attempts were made to include an anti-Sunday travelling clause into the Great Western Railway Bill. Radical MP John Roebuck felt that the attempt to introduce a clause preventing Sunday traffic in the Glasgow, Paisley & Greenock Railway Bill (1837) was one of pure hypocrisy as canals, stagecoaches and turnpikes had been in use on Sundays for decades without any complaint. He also thought that many Sabbatarians were in fact supporters of the older means of transport, and that the canals and roads would be making money on Sundays, at the expense of the newer railways. Thus, Sabbatarianism was a stalking horse for other transport interests: a matter of profits, not prophets.

Roebuck (and others) were correct in their assertions: of the nearly 1,400 coaches that were licensed to run to and from London in 1836, over 1,000 were able to do so on Sundays. In the provinces, one third of the 1,434 coaches ran on Sundays. Thus, it was not Sunday travelling *per se* that was sinful, but rather the idea of railways.

*The Times* concluded that:

> The uncharitable spirit in which railways have been treated ... is additional proof of the tendency of human nature to quarrel with all that is new, and to assume that [if] a thing is at variance with our established habits, it must be bad.

Typically, a compromise was reached: on the Liverpool & Manchester, as several directors had resigned as a response to running trains on Sundays, it was agreed that no trains would be run between 10 a.m. and 4.30 p.m. (the 'Church Interval') and careful record be made of the trains run and fares collected, so that the proceeds from those trains be transferred to a special charity fund rather than go to the company and shareholders. This fund enabled the directors to make grants, usually to help the poor and those in distress. Ultimately, the Liverpool & Manchester found Sunday travelling to be quite popular: '334 passengers went from Manchester to Liverpool, and about that number the reverse way' during the first full week of operating.

When the matter of Sunday travelling appeared on the Manchester & Leeds Railway in 1839, one of the directors, the prominent Unitarian mill-owner John Fielden, argued that as all days were holy, no single day should be singled out as holier than others, and quoted Mark 2:27: 'The Sabbath was made for man, not man for the Sabbath ...' He thought Sunday travel was not sinful, but he would not compel anyone to work on a Sunday. Fielden concluded – in a thoroughly Unitarian way – that Sunday travelling was a matter of an individual's *conscience*, and so it would be the 'passenger themselves who would be the desecrator ... *if* any desecration has taken place'.

The railway could also be a boon to the faithful. About 200 citizens of Leeds took advantage of the York & North Midland Railway in June and July 1839 to travel to York to hear an epic two-hour sermon preached by the Dean of York. The *Leeds Intelligencer* (6 July 1839) noted that 'to the credit of those who take advantage of Railway Travelling on the Sabbath', they made a point of 'attending ... both the morning and afternoon service.'

## Going by Train

We know more about the experiences of passengers travelling second and third class than we do about first, largely because of the numbers of complaints through letters to friends, the railway, to domestic press and even to Parliament. The 1843 Select Committee on Railways (rates and fares), which led to the 1844 Gladstone Act, found that 'second-class carriages are generally unprovided with windows; and the third-class carriages are, with very few exceptions, entirely open'. Furthermore, these carriages contrasted negatively with the French railways, where the Chamber of Deputies ordered that all carriages had to be roofed-in, to prevent passengers in open carriages being:

> Exposed to the assaults of the weather and rapid current of air, but also to the risk of fire from particles of burning coke thrown out by the engine.

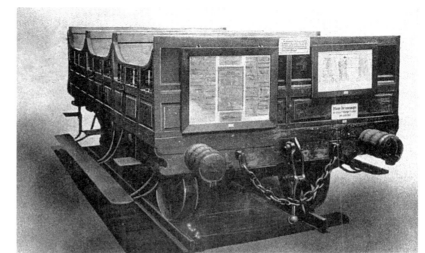

This German third-class coach is typical of the 1830s, offering absolutely no protection from the weather. Note the dumb buffers.

Similarly, in Belgium, 'no class of passenger' was to be 'exposed to the weather in carriages wholly or partially open'. Entirely open carriages were also banned in Germany. Britain appeared to be lagging woefully behind its continental neighbours in terms of passenger comfort, and in cheapness of fares.

The Railway Commissioners singled out one company in particular for condemnation:

> On the London & Birmingham Line, the only third-class train is one special train daily, each way ... [the] passengers are almost universally exposed without any protection, to the wind and rain, and to the steam, dust, and sparks from the engine, which latter are very apt to burn their clothes. There cannot be a doubt that this exposure for long journeys, or in bad weather, is frequently such as no man, and certainly no woman and child, could encounter, without risk to health ... Even in the ordinary second-class carriages, the exposure to cold and draughts is undoubtedly often sufficient to prevent persons, at all delicate, from travelling ...

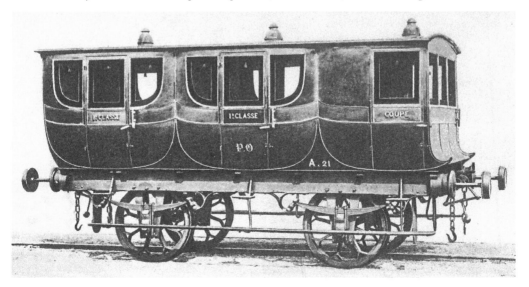

A beautiful coupé-ended first-class carriage belonging to the Chemin de Fer Paris à Orléans. A triumph of the late 1830s coachbuilder's art.

A semi-open third-class carriage from the Paris à Orleans, c. 1830s. Despite the roof, boarded-up ends and leather curtains as weather protection, there don't appear to be any springs!

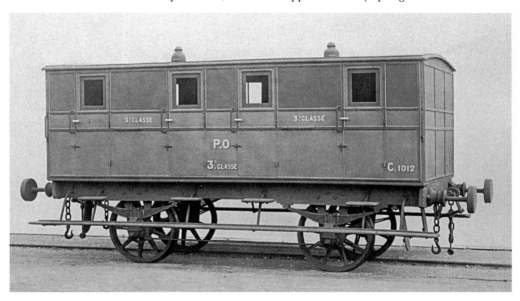

A fully enclosed third-class carriage from the Paris à Orleans, c. 1844 – far in advance of contemporary British practice. Note oil lamps, sprung buffing gear, draw gear and axles. This image bears comparison with the previous image.

No words were spared, unfortunately, for the poor guards who had to perch on the roofs of these early carriages, swaddled in greatcoats through wind, rain and snow.

Two Scotsmen, Messrs. Grainger and Buchanan, travelled on the Liverpool & Manchester on 16 and 17 September 1830. They reported:

We shall only observe, that no inconvenience whatever was felt by any of the passengers, even moving at the extraordinary rate of 20 and 25 miles an hour. The motion ... was smooth and

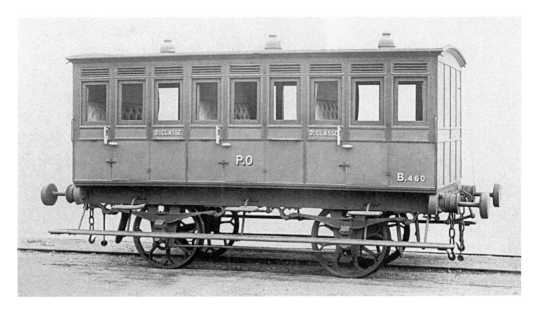

An enclosed Paris à Orleans second-class carriage: note the upholstered interior, glass windows, oil lamps and ventilators – as good as first class in Britain!

easy beyond any thing hitherto experienced on the smoothest turnpike of Mr. McAdam; so much so that we could read with the greatest of ease, and even manage to write a letter. In a very short time we became quite unconscious of the rapid motion; at the highest speed which we attained, we could observe the passengers, among whom were a good many ladies, talking to gentlemen with the utmost *sang-froid.* From all that we have observed, we should consider the rate of 25 miles an hour, on a level, or nearly level road, as perfectly practicable and safe. The only source of accident that can arise is from any sudden stoppage of the vehicles by an obstruction on the road, or by any of wheels of the carriage giving way – circumstances which are not likely to occur with ordinary care and attention.

That said, one correspondent to the *Liverpool Mercury* (22 October 1830) was quick to deny this:

It is not true that one may read and write with perfect ease and satisfaction. We may read but not very agreeably; and we may write, but not very easily, nor indeed without much difficulty.

Early travellers were far more impressed with the novelty of railway travel than any shortcomings in passenger accommodation; the actress Fanny Kemble had been overjoyed by her experience in 1830, and H. Crabb Robinson of *The Times* was suitably impressed by his travelling experiences:

We travelled in the second class of carriages. There were five carriages linked together, in each of which were placed open seats for the traveller, four and four facing each other ... There was a close carriage, also a machine for the luggage ... Everything went on so rapidly that I had scarcely the power of observation ... On setting out there is a slight jolt, arising from the chain catching on each carriage, but, once in motion, we proceeded as smoothly as possible ... The machines produces little smoke or steam...

The most remarkable movements of the journey are those when trains pass one another. The rapidity is such that there is no recognising the features of a traveller ... the noise of the passing engine was like the whizzing of a rocket.

Some of the early accounts of railway travel possess a certain *naiveté*; for example, Fanny Kemble describing *Rocket* as a mechanical horse, 'a snorting little animal', which she 'was inclined to pat'. The whole experience was 'magical … no fairy tale was ever half so wonderful'. Another traveller was equally enchanted:

> The whole passage between Liverpool & Manchester is a series of enchantments, surpassing any in the Arabian Nights, because they are realities, not fictions, yet there are certain epochs in the transit which are particularly exciting. There are the startings, the ascents, the descents, the Tunnels, the Chat Moss … at the instant of starting … the automaton belches forth an explosion of steam, and seams for a second or two quiescent. But quickly the explosions are reiterated, with shorter and shorter intervals till they are too rapid to be counted, though still distinct … they … resemble the pantings of a lion or tiger than any sound that has ever vibrated on my ear … The scene was magnificent, I would almost say terrific. Although it was a dead calm, the wind appeared to be blowing a hurricane, such was the velocity with which we darted through the air. Yet all was steady; and there was something in the precision of the machinery that inspired a degree of confidence over fear, safety over danger.

The most nerve-wracking part of the journey was when two trains met, and passed:

> The meetings or crossing of the steam trains flying in opposite directions are scarcely less agitating to the nerves than their transit through tunnels. The velocity of their course … call forth the involuntary but fearful thought of a collision, with all its horrible consequences. The period of suspense, however, thought most exquisitely painful, is but momentary: and in a few seconds the object of the terror is far out of sight behind.

Thomas Creevey MP – part of the anti-railway lobby – thought the whole experience of rail travel 'frightful … it is impossible to divest yourself of the notion of instant death', leaving him with 'a headache which has not left me yet'. One letter writer in November 1829 shared his experiences with a friend in Stafford about his trip on 'The Liverpool & Manchester Mail Road':

> We then had another ride, Mr Stephenson's beautiful prize Locomotive-engine, the 'Rocket', taking us a full mile in two minutes, without any sensation of going too fast, and so easily as to enable me to write with facility and steadiness: on looking at the roof of the carriage, no motion was perceived at all differing from an ordinary pace, and going with the wind the speed was not indicated in any unusual manner, but on looking down, the earth appeared to fly. On returning and meeting the wind, great coats were buttoned, and necks wrapped up, a smart breeze being felt. I feel assured that the most timid female will much prefer this mode of conveyance after one trial. The engine is managed by two men, and is stopped with great ease … The engines now work without smoke … passengers will be conveyed at a rate of 30 to 40 miles an hour, the fare will be about one penny per mile inside.

Another traveller wrote:

> Upon examining the internal fittings up of the carriages, upon which so much of the comfort of his journey will depend, the traveller will find that the first class carriages are divided into three entirely distinct compartments, and these compartments into six divisions (except in the mails in which there are only four) so that each traveller has an entire seat to himself, in which he can recline as freely and comfortably as in the most luxurious arm chair; and after the shades of evening have gathered over the scenery, can read the news of the day, or turn over the pages of a little volume by the light of a lamp, which is fixed in the roof of the coach.

FIRST CLASS

THIRD CLASS

RAILWAY TRAVELLING—A CONTRAST

The contrast between first and third class, as depicted by the artist from *The Graphic*.

## Second Class

As the railway became part of daily life, the novelty of rail travel soon wore off. One traveller wrote to the *Manchester Mercury* (28 September 1830), only a fortnight after the Liverpool & Manchester had opened, describing how even the first-class coaches were cold and draughty:

> At present the inside fare is seven shillings. With this I should find no fault, provided it had comfortable seats, and were sheltered from the inclemency of the weather: but this is not the case. Several friends of mine, last week, got severe colds from going to Liverpool by the above conveyance, and are now confined to their apartments; and they have come to the determination of not making a second attempt. Now, if the Directors of the company do not immediately make arrangements so as to secure the comfort and health of individuals that may travel by their carriages, they will shortly find, in place of crowded vehicles, few that will be so foolish as to go by such a conveyance where so great a risk is at stake. Another great complaint is the great inconvenience passengers are put to both in going to and from Liverpool, being set down so far from the centre of the town. Why have the directors not got offices in the centre of Liverpool and Manchester, so that people may not have the trouble of going to the commencement of the railway, and likewise vehicles of some description to convey passengers to and from the railroad, free from expense?

The lack of roofs on the open second-class carriages soon lead to:

> Many persons having complained of having their clothes burned; and no wonder when pieces of cinder, almost of a white heat, and the size of a walnut, are continuously descending among the passengers in the open carriages from the engine chimneys.

James Drake in his *Road Book of the London & Birmingham Railway* condemned:

> These cushionless, windowless, curtainless, comfortless vehicles, seem to have been purposely constructed so that the sweeping wind, enraged at being outstripped in his rapid flight, might have an opportunity of wreaking his vengeance upon the shrinking forms of their ill-fated occupants. At night, however, the partnership of the railway with Messrs. Rheumatism and Co. is dissolved, and even second-class passengers are provided with shelter from the cold and chilling blast.

Francis Coghlan offered the following advice to those travelling second-class:

> In the first place, get as far from the engine as possible – for three reasons: **First**, should an explosion take place, you may happily get off with the loss of an arm or a leg – whereas if you should happen to be placed near the said piece of hot machinery, and an unfortunate accident really occur, you would very probably be 'smashed to smithereens' ... **Secondly** – the vibration is very much diminished the further you are away from the engine. **Thirdly** – always sit (if you can get a seat) with your back towards the engine, against the boarded part of the waggon; by this plan you will avoid being chilled by a cold current of air which passes through these open waggons, and also save you from being nearly blinded by the small cinders which escape through the funnel.

Due to these complaints, the directors ordered that roofs be fitted to their second-class carriages in 1833. Yet, they were still referred to as 'travelling pneumonia wagons.' One irate passenger thought that even when fitted with roofs, the carriages were:

> Incomparably worse than if they had been open without a roof, that covering occasions such cutting currents of wind – I have not experienced rain – that the suffering is intense. They are no doubt constructed to increase the profits of the Company, by inducing the travellers to pay the first-class fares. But is it not cruel – is it not unprincipled – is it not a mockery of limited means – to offer to convey passengers for a smaller fare, only in such a manner that their health, and even their lives, are placed under great risk?

FIRST CLASS PASSENGERS.

SECOND CLASS PASSENGERS.

*Above, right and opposite*: *The Illustrated London News's* take on the different classes of travel: bourgeois (if rude) first class; cramped second class; wet and cold third.

The *Manchester Times* described them as little better than pig wagons:

> The second-class carriages ... seem to have been made as uncomfortable and unsightly as possible ... they are little better than those which are provided for the pigs ... either in point of comfort or decoration. It is true that they have a covering, but it only serves to concentrate the current of cold air and makes it doubly injurious to health.

The author, having travelled many miles as a guard in the replica 'blue coaches' at the Museum of Science & Industry, Manchester, can confirm that these coaches can be very cold, wet and miserable on anything other than bright sunny day. Rain not only blows in, but is channelled onto the passenger by the roofs, with the driest seats being those in the middle of the coach. Those at either end, however, can be extremely cold and wet. The travellers in the 1830s going second class from Liverpool or Manchester must have been of a hardy sort, and their complaints are certainly justified.

Thomas Normington, who would become a senior member of staff on the Lancashire & Yorkshire Railway, recalled travelling in one of these open carriages between Dewsbury and Manchester:

> The carriage was simply a square wood box or wagon, without seats or roof, and exposed to all sorts of weather, and the passengers wedged in, like cattle ... Of course going to see my Grandfather, I must go in my Sunday clothes, and had on a new top hat. To my surprise and sorrow, upon emerging out of Summit Tunnel, I found my new top hat entirely spoiled, the down being fizzled up by the small hot cinders emitted from the funnel of the engine ... On my return home I again travelled by train in a stand-up box from Manchester to Thornhill, in a down pour of rain the whole of the journey. This, and the previous frizzle, completely put an end to my brand-new hat. In those days, people were not so well educated in extortionate habits, otherwise a claim would have been made for a new hat upon the railway company.

In March 1841, Thomas Fielden, a director of the Manchester & Leeds, argued in favour of improving the lot of third- and second-class passengers, but this was met with scorn and derision by the Board: improved conditions might draw passengers away from comfortable first class!

A lack of raised platforms on the Liverpool & Manchester was the cause of the following incident in the winter of 1842:

> At the Broad Green Station ... a female of enormous obesity, quite an African Venus, made her appearance to fill the empty stall [in the carriage]. The guards being occupied somewhere else, the Liverpool gentlemen next to the door took hold of her hand that was stretched in assistance; the task, however, was above the limits of his dragging power; the lady with a good grasp and a heavy pull tumbled back, taking her cavalier with her on a heap of snow, where both were ... extended, no serious mischief being the consequence. Now, three men backing her centre of gravity, she was at last hoisted into the vehicle, and all was right save the loss of ten minutes.

Long-suffering passengers on the London & Birmingham, which ran semi-open 'day seconds' into the mid-1840s, agreed with the sentiments of the travellers on the Liverpool & Manchester:

> [There is] serious risk and inconvenience which second-class passengers have to endure while travelling in the abominable open carriages which are used on the London and Birmingham. The North Midland have certainly improved their carriages of late; but they are quite dark, and when closed seem more suited to the conveyance of criminals than for honest, independent, Englishmen. I write these few lines, however, and I may mention the very comfortable and superior second-class carriages which have lately been put upon the Manchester and Leeds. I think if other companies would follow this example, I think the public would have no occasion to complain. I am quite convinced that great numbers are driven into the first-class in consequence of the great danger of taking severe colds while exposed to the dreadful currents of air ... in the open carriages. I hope ... in any future Act ... a clause will be inserted that second-class carriages shall have closed sides and glass windows, similar to those recently put on the Manchester and Leeds line.

The enclosed, upholstered first-class compared to the 'travelling pneumonic wagons' of second class on the Liverpool & Manchester. (Duncan Hough)

An inhabitant of Coventry also hoped that the example of the Manchester & Leeds, which had introduced glazed windows to their second-class coaches, would spur the London & Birmingham to upgrade their second-class accommodation:

> And give the public the benefit in their second-class carriages, which have had merely a cover on the top, and that being of very little use in wet and cold weather, except to a few favoured individuals, to get into the centre. If the Manchester & Leeds Company can afford to indulge the public, surely the London & Birmingham Company may venture. It is deplorable to witness the starved condition which persons leave the carriages in winter.

> (*Coventry Herald*, 29 September 1843)

Another outraged passenger writing to the *Birmingham Journal* (11 May 1839) called them 'injurious receptacles':

> Made as uncomfortable as possible ... I have no doubt that many will have to date, not only loss of health, but loss of life through travelling on them. In the present month of May, I speak from experience, they are very much worse than travelling outside a coach in severely cold weather.

In his evidence before a Parliamentary Select Committee, Robert Sharp of Lichfield described second- and third-class open carriages as 'endangering health', as the passengers 'suffer very much from cold, and the rain beating in'. One of his fellow travellers could stand it no longer and at Wolverton 'paid the higher price to go by first'. The seconds of George Hudson's North Midland Railway also came in for censure:

> I have been on almost all the railways in the Kingdom; but the second-class carriages of the North Midland are the most uncomfortable of all the others. Now I would advise those that cannot afford to pay first-class fares by no means to take the second-class, unless they either intend to be starved to death, or catch some incurable cold, for nobody that has not experienced it can have any idea of the draft through the carriages, and the extreme cold when there are either head or side winds;

and if it rains, it blows through you ... the third-class carriages are infinitely more comfortable ... Besides you have the opportunity of hold up an umbrella which you have not in the other.

(Sheffield Independent, 3 December 1842)

## Gladstone's Act

Ultimately, enough was enough, resulting in the Gladstone Act (1844), which stated that third-class passengers had to travel in an enclosed vehicle provided with seats, running at average speed of more than 12 mph and at a cost of 1*d* per mile. Some companies, such as the Great Western, took this to extremes, constructing what appeared to be prison cells on rails, while others built new enclosed third-class vehicles and downgraded their existing open- or semi-open carriages to fourth class.

Robert Ritchie complained two years after the passing of the Act that many companies had taken the letter of the law literally, creating fully enclosed vehicles with tiny windows (if any at all, which barely admitted light or air), into which third-class passengers were crammed like cattle:

> Third-class carriages are so hideous and dismal, air and light being nearly both excluded, that they are more adapted for carriage of prisoners than passengers. In some of the third class government carriages there is a wax cloth curtain to draw over the opening, or rather hole, left on both sides of the carriage ... Why should not glazed windows be in every carriage? It cannot be at expense of glass; and a penny per mile is surely sufficient to cover such expenses and pay the railway company properly, and when night trains are used they should be properly lighted.

In the opinion of many, the Great Western was by far the worst offender in its provision of second-class accommodation, let alone third:

> Their second-class carriages were merely pens, railed-off after the fashion of pens for cattle, without any protection from wind and whatever, except so far as they are boarded as high as the loins of persons in them. All above are open rails.

(Manchester Courier, 6 March 1841)

Replica Great Western broad-gauge semi-open second-class and standing-only third-class coaches of the 1840s, behind replica *Iron Duke*.

Then there was the question of through-running between different companies. The North Union Railway operated fully enclosed second-class coaches from the start, and as a result asked the directors of the Liverpool & Manchester whether their second-class ticket holders could use Liverpool & Manchester first-class coaches. The answer was a resounding no: North Union second-class passengers would have to exchange their enclosed vehicles for the semi-opens of the Liverpool & Manchester. The same was true of the London & Birmingham and North Midland:

> We have observed remonstrances addressed to the officers at Derby ... in consequence of this company having no enclosed second-class carriages, passengers by the London and Birmingham and Midland Counties, are turned out from their safe and comfortable enclosed and sashed second-class carriages, into one wholly without any side protection whatever; and that, too, at two or three o'clock in the morning ... The London & Birmingham, as far as the second-class carriages used by day are concerned are open boxes – those for the night are unexceptionable; but it is frequently after eleven o'clock at night before the so-called day carriages arrive at their destination.
>
> (*Manchester Courier*, 6 March 1841)

To add insult to injury, once the Midland Counties had introduced its fully enclosed seconds, the London & Birmingham – over whose line the Midland Counties had running rights – informed them:

> In [an] offensive manner ... that their enclosed second-class carriages should *not* come upon the London and Birmingham line, on account of the contrast it would draw to their own *inferior accommodation*, and the prejudice and discontent it would create in the public mind. The Derby and Birmingham were obliged to obey.
>
> (*Manchester Courier*, 6 March 1841)

The plight of second- and especially third-class passengers was even commented upon from the Pulpit, one Minister in London preaching upon 'Blessed is he that considereth the poor' to condemn the treatment of less affluent railway travellers.

The London & Birmingham not only treated its second-class passengers poorly, but the lateness of its trains, rudeness of its staff and low-quality refreshments were duly noted in a letter to *The Times* in January 1839:

> We arrived at last at Birmingham, at half past 1, exactly *two hours and a half behind our time*, the proper time for the train's arrival being 11 o'clock. Here we were told that there would not be an instant's delay, and that if we left our places for a moment, it should be at the extremely probably risk of behind left behind. We had been seven hours and a half on the journey, exposed for one hour of that period to a biting blast upon the moor. The 'creature comforts' were eagerly desiderated by us all, refreshment would have been more refreshing: but the peremptory mandate which had been given to us, and the dread of losing our places, chained us to our seats Positively as the announcement was made that there should not be an instant's delay, 10, 15 minutes passed, and we all the time subjected to the tortures of Tanatalus, with the Railway Hotel within 40 yards of us, and mocking visions of all sorts of viands and pleasing potions – hunger knowing at our vitals, and plenty of 'grub' in view – We roared out for messengers to bring refreshments to us for several minutes, in vain. At length, a knavish Porter came to our assistance, and brought us glasses of muddy ale for which he charged us 6*d* a piece; and coarse lumps of bread, with the most unsavoury pieces of fat bacon superimposed thereon, without one particle of mustard – a travesty upon sandwiches – and for these 1s was *freely paid*, and accordingly we devoured them eagerly ... In spite of the impudent, lying announcement, that there should not be a moment's delay, we did not leave Birmingham until seven minutes past 2 – 37 minutes after our arrival! ...

The irregularities which occur upon this line of railway are so frequent and so altogether eccentric. Varying from half an hour to three and even four hours beyond the stated period, that punctuality, the first essential of business, and no mean ingredient of pleasure, is absolutely laughed to scorn by a self-sufficient batch of monopolists.

Another traveller described the pork pies served at the Wolverton refreshment room as 'a pink, shuddering, glistening mass encased in a pastry which would break even the finest teeth', doubting very much if the contents were indeed porcine. The lukewarm coffee had been, the writer mused, brewed from a single bean.

The situation for passengers on the London & Birmingham route, especially those travelling second-class, led to enterprising stagecoach owners running coaches between London and Birmingham, offering better reliability and better comfort than the railway company would offer, making up for lost time with a more pleasant travelling experience.

Then as now, overloaded and delayed trains were the norm at Christmas. On the Liverpool & Manchester, during its first winter of operations (1830–1831: the coldest in fifteen years) one train was delayed by five hours because the Planet Class locomotive's single driving wheels could not find a grip on the icy railhead. Pity the poor passengers stranded in unheated carriages, with no food or drink (other than that which they might have brought with them) and no means to relieve themselves, or the train crew – and especially the guards – exposed to the elements in a recorded ambient temperature of -12°C!

*The Morning Post* (30 December 1843) reported:

There is generally at Christmas more than the ordinary amount of traffic on the Liverpool & Manchester Railroad; but on Saturday the number of passengers was so great that the Up-trains did not arrive at Manchester until an hour or more beyond their usual time; in the evening, the Up-trains were later still. Many trains departing leaving would-be passengers stranded upon the platforms.

Thus, within mere years of the railways opening, overcrowding, delays, poor customer service and over-priced, low-quality eatables were already an accepted norm of going by rail.

*Lion* – the sole surviving Liverpool & Manchester locomotive – with replica second- and first-class coaches. Being a 'luggage engine', *Lion* would never have worked passenger trains.

# Conclusion

In just eight years, the railways had transformed the travelling experience; more people could travel further and for less cost than ever before.

The railway carriage developed rapidly from the horse-drawn stagecoach on rails of the Stockton & Darlington of 1825, to the lavishly appointed first-class carriages of the Worsdells on the Liverpool & Manchester – a design that was so successful it was copied by many of the early railway companies, both at home and abroad. Success of the railway companies, however, did not necessarily mean that passengers were better taken care of, especially anyone who could not afford to go first class.

Second-class, let alone third-class passengers did not figure highly on the Liverpool & Manchester, or later, on the London & Birmingham's list of priorities. The Liverpool & Manchester had taken some early steps to improve the travel experience of second-class passengers by providing roofs and boarding up the open ends of the carriages, but they remained crude, cold and uncomfortable. Other companies, such as the Manchester & Leeds and Midland Counties, which ran through heavily populated industrialising regions, saw second and especially third (and fourth!) class as lucrative business, providing for the latter rudimentary standing-only accommodation without 'a particle of protection' for the occupants.

Companies such as the London & Birmingham recognised that they had a monopoly on rail travel north out of London and could therefore dictate their own terms to their passengers, and to other companies that either connected with, or had running rights over, their line. Their attitude towards second class appears to have been one of, 'If you think this is bad, try the stagecoach.' Indeed, treatment of second class on the London & Birmingham lead to a resurgence in stagecoach travel. The situation became so bad for anyone other than the first-class traveller that Parliament had to intervene with the Regulation of Railways Act 1844 (the Gladstone Act), which specified minimum standards of service for the poorest rail traveller.

Was rail travel in the 1830s better or worse than in 2017? In terms of speed and safety, the answer is definitely in favour of 2017: steel-bodied vehicles, running on bogies, with brakes (considered an optional extra in 1838) and automatic doors compared to short, wooden-bodied, wooden-framed slam-door stock. In 2017, every train has a lavatory and long-distance trains do at least provide some form of on-board refreshment from an airline-style 'at seat' trolley service. Trains are cleaner than before and there is no danger of getting your clothes burned by falling ashes. In 1838, because passengers booked twenty-four hours in advance, they were guaranteed a seat – just like today's 'advanced booking' – but usually only in first class.

Perhaps the overcrowding, jostling, standing-all-the-way experience of the modern-day commuter is not that different from over 170 years ago. Indeed, while the 'masses went forth' crammed together, the first-class passenger still enjoys the luxury of a seat, less noise and complimentary food and drink (something their 1838 counterpart would have had to provide for themselves).

For the average passenger, however, the travelling experience of 2017 and 1838 are probably not that different.

# Select Bibliography

## Newspapers and Journals

*Coventry Herald*
*Edinburgh Courant*
*Liverpool Mercury*
*Manchester Courier*
*Manchester Guardian*
*Manchester Times*
*Morning Post*
*Railway Times*
*Sheffield Independent*
*The Times*

## Books

Anon, *The Grand Junction and the Liverpool and Manchester Railway Companion* (London: S. Cornish, 1837).
Brees, S. C., *Railway Practice*, second edition (London: John Williams, 1838).
Brees, S. C., *Second Series: Railway Practice* (London: John Williams & Co., 1840).
Brees, S.C., *Third Series: Railway Practice* (London: John Williams & Co., 1848).
Brees, S. C., *Railway Practice* (London: Griffin & Co., 1859).
Clarke, D. K., *Railway Machinery* (London: Blackie, 1855).
Coghlan, F., *The Iron Road Book and Railway Companion* (London: A. H. Bailey & Co., 1838).
Dempsey, G. C., *The Practical Railway Engineer* (London: John Weale, 1855).
Drake, J., *Drake's Road Book of the London & Birmingham Railway* (London: Haywood & Moore, 1838).
Freeling, A., *The London and Birmingham Railway Companion* (London: Whittaker & Co., 1838).
Head, F. B., *Stokers and Pokers: Or, The London and North-Western Railway* (London: John Murray, 1849).
Mogg, E., *Mogg's Hand-book for Railway Travellers* (London: Edward Mogg, 1840).
Normington, T., *The Lancashire & Yorkshire Railway* (Manchester: John Heywood, 1898).
Walker, J. S., *An Accurate Description of the Liverpool and Manchester Railway* (Liverpool: 1830).
Wishaw, F., *The Railways of Great Britain and Ireland* (London: John Weale, 1841).
Wood. N., *A Practical Treatise on Railroads* (1838).